WILLIE NELSON'S LETTERS TO AMERICA

Willie Nelson
with Turk Pipkin

HARPER
HORIZON

Published by Harper Horizon, an imprint of HarperCollins Focus LLC.

Any internet addresses, phone numbers, or company or product information printed in this book are offered as a resource and are not intended in any way to be or to imply an endorsement by Harper Horizon, nor does Harper Horizon vouch for the existence, content, or services of these sites, phone numbers, companies, or products beyond the life of this book.

ISBN 978-0-7852-4155-3 (eBook)
ISBN 978-0-7852-4154-6 (HC)

Library of Congress Control Number: 2021930698

Printed in the United States of America
21 22 23 24 25   LSC   10 9 8 7 6 5 4 3 2 1

CONTENTS

CONTENTS

CONTENTS

INTRODUCTION

Dear Readers,

Thanks for picking up a copy of my new book, a collection of fond memories, personal letters, good songs, and bad jokes. These are stories that start back when I was a kid in Abbott, Texas, and reach forward to the current pandemic, which has us locked up at home singing our own versions of "Hello Walls."

It's been a long time since I wrote, "Shotgun Willie sits around in his underwear," but it don't seem like all that much has changed. Just ask my wife, Annie. The song of the year for married couples ought to be "How Can I Miss You When You Never Go Anywhere?"

One good thing about the lockdown is this eighty-seven-year-old guitar picker has had time to write out a few of the stories that made me who I am, and to think about what I'd like to say to people I love, and to some I loved who aren't with us anymore. I've also written to people I've admired or who've inspired me along the way.

I've always been a letter writer. I spent a lot of my life on the road, so I sent notes to family to say things I couldn't say in person. When I was young, I was taught to write thank-you letters. I could spend the rest of my life writing thank-you notes to friends, family, and my heroes, but I'd still end up leaving out someone I love. So I'll say it now.

Thank you. Every one of you. If you're wondering if I mean you, the answer is, "Yes, I do."

There is nothing more important than family and friends, so this book is dedicated to all of you. I know you accept me as I am. For those who don't know me as well, if some of my thoughts don't hit a home run with you, you should at least know that they come from my heart. Differences are to be expected in life, especially in difficult times. Despite our differences, this is a time when remembering our common bonds and dreams has the power to bring us all back together again.

I've done a fair amount of rough and rocky traveling, so I guess this is the good, the bad, and the funny. Like those jokes I mentioned, life is better when we don't take it too seriously.

Speaking of which . . .

"What do you call a guitar player without a girlfriend?"

"Homeless."

If you don't think that's funny, you probably don't know many guitar players.

Okay, where was I? Oh yeah . . . letters! We all know the art of letter scribbling ain't what it used to be. And grammar ain't either. Back when you had to write or type something with your own hand, mail it halfway across the country, then wait for a reply, there was reason to invest a lot of thought into your letters. If you were good at it, those letters were like carefully crafted songs. That art has been replaced by the instant exchanges of texting, and even though I'm a champion thumb-typer, there are some things that don't fit in the length of a tweet.

My songwriting and producer pal Buddy Cannon and I often write songs by text, sending verses and choruses back and forth like teenagers making plans for Saturday night. That may sound crazy, but don't knock success unless you've tried it. It's a system that's worked for us for years, and the lyrics to a few of those songs are in this book. I'm also including lyrics for some of my classic songs and a few stories about how I wrote, sold, or recorded them.

I'm working on a new song now, but so far I only have two lines:

If you don't leave me alone
I'll find someone who will

I don't know where that one's headed. But I'll keep you posted.

I once wrote a song called "Who'll Buy My Memories?" And I guess I'm about to find that out. So, without any more jabber-jaw, here are my songs, my stories, and my letters to America. And a few bad jokes.

WHO'LL BUY MY MEMORIES?

by Willie Nelson

A past that's sprinkled with the blues
A few old dreams that I can't use
Who'll buy my mem'ries
Of things that used to be

There were the smiles before the tears
And with the smiles some better years
Who'll buy my mem'ries
Of things that used to be

When I remember how things were
My memories all leave with her
I'd like to start my life anew
But memories just make me blue

A cottage small just built for two
A garden wall with violets blue
Who'll buy my mem'ries
Of things that used to be

Dear America,

This is your old friend, Willie, sending a note to see how you're doing and to say I'm doing fine. I've long believed in the positive idea of being fine and being committed to a goal of always moving forward. If I'm backing up, it's just to get a running start. Those are words you can live by.

But when times get tough for family and friends—and I like to think of everyone around the world as my family and friends—I sometimes look back on songs I've written that might contain some wisdom or maybe a laugh that still applies today. I once wrote a country song called "Three Days," about the three toughest days of heartbreak—yesterday, today, and tomorrow. So I guess I'm thinking now about lessons I learned yesterday that would apply today and tomorrow.

When the going gets tough and the tough need a little inspiration to get going, I think about another of my songs.

Lord, please give me a sign
For these are difficult times

These really are difficult times. As for me, I'm getting bored to all hell sitting at home and wishing I was on the road making music with my friends. But my problems are small potatoes compared to many millions of people who don't know where their next paycheck is coming from or how they're gonna feed their families.

I was born during your Great Depression of the 1930s, so I had some early experience with hard times. My sister, Bobbie, and I were raised by our grandparents. After my granddaddy died, times were even tougher. For Thanksgiving dinner one year, we split a can of soup! Some may not think of those as the good old days, but my grandmother, who we called Mama, was always there for us. It took love and faith and music to carry us through.

Even today, I can hear my grandmother's voice and her fingers on the piano keys as she played and sang "Old Rugged Cross" and Woody Guthrie's great anthem to America, "This Land Is Your Land." The hard times made us strong, and the good times made us stronger. Together, they made me who I am.

Now here we are, America, eight decades later, and just like the old song, hard times have come again once more. Once again, we are trying to hold to each other and hold to your great American dream for every person. We're trying to find what unites us—to remember our shared beliefs in family, in love, and in your democratic ideals, so we can come through as a stronger America. If we don't find what unites us, we will once again be a house divided. We tried that once in the 1860s, and six hundred thousand Americans died fighting against each other. That should be our reminder that we need to get our shit together and remember the ways we are alike rather than focusing on the ways we're different.

When our nation was in mourning after 9/11, you gave me the opportunity to do my part for the live concert *America: A Tribute to Heroes*. That inspiring event had one of the largest audiences in television history. I followed a string of great artists—Bruce Springsteen, Tom Petty, Alicia Keys, and many more. Then I got to lead everyone in an inspiring rendition of your beautiful song, "America the Beautiful." As we sang onstage that evening, I felt that I could hear the television audience singing, too, a nationwide chorus raising our voices from sea to shining sea.

To sum it all up, I'd like to amplify across America the words of Dr. Martin Luther King Jr., "Let freedom ring!"

From a hilltop in Texas,

Willie Nelson

I wrote this song when I was in a bar with my friend Zeke Varnon. An old drunk came up and asked for some money. He said, "I ain't had nothin' to drink in three days: yesterday, today, and tomorrow." I gave him some money, laughed, and wrote this song.

THREE DAYS

by Willie Nelson

Three days that I dread to see arrive
Three days that I hate to be alive
Three days filled with tears and sorrow
Yesterday, today, and tomorrow

There are three days I know that I'll be blue
Three days that I'll always dream of you
And it does no good to wish these days would end
'Cause the same three days start over again

Three days that I dread to be alive
Three days that I hate to see arrive
Three days filled with tears and sorrow
Yesterday, today, and tomorrow

There are three days I know that I'll be blue
Three days that I'll always dream of you
And it does no good to wish these days would end
'Cause the same three days start over again

Three days that I dread to see arrive
Three days that I hate to be alive
Three days filled with tears and sorrow
Yesterday, today, and tomorrow

Dear Mama and Daddy,

I hope you forgive me for taking so long to write. I also hope this letter finds you both in your "shining city on a hill," though I suspect the heaven you've found is on a prairie with a white-framed house and a porch, a guitar, and a piano. You were my grandparents, but you raised Sister and me, and the names Mama and Daddy were perfect for you.

Sometimes when I slow down and pay close attention, I can feel Daddy placing my hands on the frets of that first guitar he gave me when I was just six. It was only a Stella from the Sears & Roebuck catalog, but to me it was the world. Daddy, you taught me how to play the D, A, and G chords, the building blocks of country music. And look what happened. You were a big man, and I remember your bass voice singing, "Where have you been, Billy Boy?" I remember you working hard in your blacksmith shop. After the flu and pneumonia took you, those chords and that music have never been far from my side. Neither have you.

And Mama, if I close my eyes, I can still hear you singing, "Rock of ages, cleft for me." I'd give about anything to really hear your voice again, and for you to see how me and Sister Bobbie turned out. For Bobbie is a glorious wonder, as beautiful now as she was as a girl, and filled with the spirit of music and love that you gave to us both.

After Daddy died—with me just six and Sister Bobbie only nine—you never let us doubt that there were good things ahead for us. Whenever hard times found me, I remembered the examples you set and the lessons you taught me. I still do.

Truly the Nelson family has been blessed. I've had eight wonderful kids and a whole bunch of grandkids and great-grandkids, and I'm proud as buttons of every one. I don't know if you can see them all, but I see you in all of them. Daddy too. My friend and teacher Reverend Taliaferro used to say there is no such thing as death. When I look at all the Nelson generations that still carry the two of you with them, I know that it's true.

You taught me a lot, and I've tried to pass some of that to my family. Back in Abbott—at home, at school, and when I worked in the fields—I learned the importance of believing we could do anything we wanted to do. If we worked hard enough, you said, we could become whoever we dreamed of being.

I dreamed of being a songwriter and musician, but I also knew that I wanted to be surrounded by family. You instilled that in me, and though my parents were young and didn't stay together, I came to know their love as well.

Each in their own way, my kids have carried on our family traditions of music and love. As America recently committed to staying at home for the general health of all, I've been fortunate to hunker down at my home outside of Austin, with my wife, Annie, and our sons, Lukas and Micah. The boys have their own bands and have toured with me and many others. They miss being on the road just like I do, but in the evenings, when we pull out our guitars, we pass the hours playing and singing our favorite songs. And we all know this extended time together is a blessing.

Sixty years ago, when times were hard for me, I went to see my mother at her new home in Oregon. While I was there, I started writing a song that sprung from you, Mama and Daddy, and from that little frame house in Abbott, Texas. The song I wrote in Portland was probably the first truly good and lasting song I'd ever written. And it was called "Family Bible."

Last night, Lukas, Micah, and I played and sang "Family Bible," their Nelson voices harmonizing with mine, and I guess with yours too. What more could I ask for?

And it all started from you.

Love from Luck, lucky in love,

Your boy Willie

FAMILY BIBLE

by Willie Nelson

There's a family Bible on the table
Its pages worn and hard to read
But the family Bible on the table
Will ever be my key to memories

At the end of day when work was over
And when the evening meal was done
Dad would read to us from the family Bible
And we'd count our many blessings one by one

I can see us sittin' round the table
When from the family Bible Dad would read
And I can hear my mother softly singing
Rock of ages, rock of ages cleft for me

Now this old world of ours is full of trouble
This old world would also better be
If we'd find more Bibles on the tables
And mothers singing rock of ages cleft for me

I can see us sittin' round the table
When from the family Bible Dad would read
And I can hear my mother softly singing
Rock of ages, rock of ages cleft for me

Dear Sister,

Everyone calls you Bobbie, but only I get to call you Sister.

I never loved you more than when we sat in the yard of our house in Abbott and you ate the mud pies I made for you. We were little then, and man we ate a lot of mud, you and me, so some of our love came right out of that American prairie soil.

I never loved you more than when you held my hand when we were walking to the cotton fields to work, knowing that our fingers would be bleeding by the time we came home. We were too young to be there, but we both knew we needed those few dollars a day. I liked the music from the Black, Mexican, and Czech farmworkers, but I wanted out of those fields, and I wanted you out of them too. We didn't even know we were poor back then. And maybe we weren't that poor after all, for we always had each other.

I never loved you more than when you played that first piano Mama bought, and I sat close as you told me what chord and what key you were playing in. Or later when I got to sit beside you and play along on my Stella guitar. You were a natural musician from the beginning, and I never would have become the musician I am without you.

I never loved you more than when you finally joined my band, and we truly became the Willie Nelson Family Band. You were part of the reason that everyone who's played in the band are truly family. We are living proof of the unforeseeable and guaranteed value of families holding their bonds to each other.

I never loved you more than the thousands of times in front of millions of people when you play your beautiful piano version of "Down Yonder." Your syncopated fingers tickle the ivories and lift every one of our audience members while I catch my breath, wipe my brow, and decide what song we'll play to kick us into high gear for the second half of the show.

It hasn't been that long since you and I returned to Abbott, Texas, to rededicate the Methodist church where we used to sing. That old steepled church, built way back in 1883, had fallen into disrepair, and the old rugged cross was looking a little too rugged.

I never loved you more than that Sunday afternoon when you and our Oklahoma pal, Leon Russell, played the first service in the newly restored church. You had pitched in with me to help put it right, and every pew and every heart was full that day. I can still hear you and Leon joining me on "Precious Memories," "I'll Fly Away," and "Amazing Grace." When we play "Amazing Grace" together, I'm reminded that all songs are, in their own way, gospel songs.

I never loved you more than all those times I showed up at your door with musicians I'd recorded with all night, or golf pals I'd played with all day. There was always a gang of us, and your kitchen smelled of pots of fresh coffee and plates of sausage and homemade biscuits and gravy. You always had a platter of fresh-sliced watermelon waiting for us too. You didn't have to, but you always looked after your little brother. And whenever you need me, I'll always look after you.

I never loved you more than when we needed each other. We always have. And we always will.

With love, your baby brother and big brother all at once,

HEALING HANDS OF TIME

by Willie Nelson

They're working while I'm missing you
Those healing hands of time
And soon they'll be dismissing you
From this heart of mine

They'll lead me safely through the night
And I'll follow as though blind
My future tightly clutched within
Those healing hands of time

They let me close my eyes just then
Those healing hands of time
And soon they'll let me sleep again
Those healing hands of time

So already I've reached mountain peaks
And I've just begun to climb
I'll get over you by clinging to
Those healing hands of time

I'll get over you by clinging to
Those healing hands of time

BOOGER RED GETS WITH IT

Before I get my letter-writing muscles fully warmed up, I'd better tell you a bit more about where I came from and why I still go back to my little hometown. I guess I'm giving you the skinny on when I really was skinny.

Some people might've said the Nelson family was dirt poor, but I know that being born in Abbott in a family that believed in music was the best possible start for Willie Hugh Nelson. When I wasn't making music or trying to make some money, me and my pals roamed the streets and fields of Abbott looking for adventures and usually finding misadventures. We'd tie a string to a purse and leave it on the highway till a driver stopped to pick it up, and then we'd snatch it back! That was always good for a laugh.

We made paddles and swatted at swarms of bumblebees till they stung us so much our eyes swelled shut. We'd sneak behind a barn and try to smoke cedar bark, coffee grounds, or corn silk. Maybe we thought we were cool, but I suspect we just wanted to break the rules.

People didn't start calling me an outlaw till I was forty years old, but I'm pretty sure that back in Abbott, I was an outlaw in training. That doesn't mean I broke a bunch of laws, but I wouldn't say I gave them a lot of thought either.

When we weren't causing trouble or playing football or basketball, my pals and I were practicing our joke telling. I became a fan of *Reader's Digest* magazine, which had two pages in the middle called "Laughter, the Best Medicine." Then I'd tell jokes like:

> "It was raining cats and dogs!"
> "How could you tell?"
> "I stepped in a poodle!"

We joked about the population of Abbott, which never seemed to change. Whenever a baby was born, we said, someone left town.

Soon we were telling jokes that you'd never hear at school or in church.

> You heard about the sign on the whorehouse door?
> It says, "We're closed. Beat it."

I thought that kind of joke was hilarious. And I guess I haven't grown up much, 'cause I still think it's funny. If you don't like it, I guess you can beat it.

My nickname was Booger Red, a name I earned at age five for my first stage performance. I was supposed to recite a poem, but I was nervous and picked my nose till it bled all over my white sailor suit. That made me mad, so I made up my own poem for the crowd.

> *What are you looking at me for?*
> *I ain't got nothin' to say*

If you don't likes the looks of me
You can look some other way

If a bloody sailor suit didn't dissuade me from performing, I guess nothing else would.

I liked to hang out at the Abbott general store, where the old men played dominoes for fifty cents a game. When one of the men got up to go somewhere, they'd have me sit in and play their dominoes. If I made a mistake, they'd yell and throw shit at me, so I learned to play pretty good.

I started writing songs in grade school, penning songs about drinking and cheating. One of the songs was called "Hangover Blues."

You can keep yo rotgut whiskey
You can keep yo gin and rye
I'll quit waking up with headaches
And a wishing I could die
Don't want no hangover blues
You can keep yo hangover blues

I didn't even know what I was writing about, so it must have been the beginning of my belief in reincarnation. Maybe I came here knowing some things before I even knew what I knew.

When I was ten years old, I wrote down a dozen of my songs and bound them into a little book and made a cover that said "Songs by Willie Nelson." I can still remember the words to those songs, so I must have been doing something right, because I can't remember what I had for breakfast this morning.

My interest in music expanded greatly when I was out working the fields picking cotton or baling hay, while watching someone drive by in a fancy Cadillac. That's what I call double motivation.

Even as a kid, I had a drive to perform, and I played my guitar anywhere they'd let me. Before I was a teenager, I started playing in a Bohemian dance band called the Rejcek Family Polka Band. Like my granddad, John Rejcek had a blacksmith shop in Abbott. I think he had sixteen children himself, all of them musicians. We played dance music—polkas and waltzes. I only had my acoustic guitar, which could hardly be heard, but it felt just right to be on a bandstand, and I knew that was what I wanted to do. The fact that I actually got paid didn't hurt either.

One gig led to another. Sister Bobbie started playing piano in a band called Bud Fletcher and the Texans. She later married the band leader, but it was already a family band because I played guitar, and my dad, Ira, would join us and play fiddle, and a guy named Whistle Watson played drums. I was barely a teenager, but I was also doing shows at KHBR Radio in Hillsboro. I didn't give up on high school or sports, but I already saw myself as a professional musician.

Seems like I made a lot of friends in all those places. You can't have too many friends, unless maybe you win the lottery and all your friends call at once to ask for money. But let's face it: you ain't gonna win the lottery. That's not even gambling. Playing the lottery is just giving your money away. But every time you make a dear friend, that's like winning the lottery anyway.

My schoolyard pal Jackie Clement took the long vacation this summer. Me and Jackie played basketball and football together, and he married a beautiful girl named Fay Dell, who both Jackie and I once admired. I used to say the only reason Jackie landed her instead of me was that he was driving a pickup and I was afoot. After seventy years of marriage, I'd say she made a good choice.

The point is, you can't make old friends. One of my best friends from the old days was Zeke Varnon. The things I learned from Zeke have carried me far, so there'll be more to come about Zeke, who I dearly loved.

DEAR ABBOTT,

I'm not that far away, but I miss you. And I guess I should be fair and say I miss Abbott, Hillsboro, and Hill County, as my home spans the greater Hill County metroplex.

You've always been good to me, and you helped me grow up fast. I learned a lot in my early years on your dirt streets. I wasn't much taller than a mailbox when my learning specialties were smokin', drinkin', and cussin'. But I also learned that a winner never quits, and a quitter never wins. And I ain't quit yet.

I'm laying low right now, so I miss having fun with my pals. I miss walking down your little streets and getting a smile and a "hiya" from every person I pass. And I miss singing with Sister in the Methodist church.

The day we reopened the church, I told the jam-packed crowd, "Sister Bobbie and I have been going to this church since we were born. I don't know what persuasion y'all were when you entered this door, but now you're all members of Abbott Methodist Church."

After the service, the community spilled out into your summer sun for an organic, farm-to-table Sunday lunch, and everything just felt right with the world.

We've grown old together, you and me, but we haven't grown apart, and we haven't changed that much either. The original Nelson family house didn't survive the decades, so my Abbott home is Doc Sims's old house. He delivered me into this world, and it feels good to keep his home looking sharp the way we all like it.

I was touched when you put up a billboard to commemorate our long relationship, but I don't need a billboard in my honor (and I hope you weren't offended when me and Zeke tried to burn it down). Naming the unpaved road to Hillsboro as Willie Nelson Road turned out to be a better fit, even if there's no sign because people keep stealing it!

We don't need signs and billboards to know we love each other. You're in my heart—both the town and the people in it. So until I'm able to spend another night in Doc's old house, keep being good to one another, hold your faith in America, and raise a little hell on Saturday night in my honor.

I'll be there as quick as I can,

THE WILLIE HUSTLE

L et's talk about hustling! I learned early that there are lots of ways to make a few bucks. And a lot of ways to lose a few. A hustler is the one who ends up on the right side of the equation. The money is always there—it's just a matter of whose pockets it's in.

I mentioned my pal Zeke Varnon. Zeke was a hustler. He also was the best domino player I ever saw. Dominoes is one of the greatest games in gambling. The game is just numbers. There are only twenty-eight dominoes, and most of them are right in front of you while you're playing.

"Take all counts and kill all doubles," Zeke taught me, which means score when you can, and if you don't have one of the seven doubles, assume the other players do, then block out those plays.

Over the years, me and Zeke played partners dominoes against the best in the world. That included a casino show match in Vegas against showboat gambler Amarillo Slim and his partner, at my friend Benny Binion's Horseshoe Casino. I lost $10,000 because Slim had someone looking over my shoulder who was silently signaling which dominoes I had. The funny thing is, I figured they'd try to cheat, but I also thought me and Zeke were so good, we'd win anyway.

Zeke also was great at poker, pool—you name it, he played it and played it well. We met when I was just a teenager playing music at the bars and clubs between Hillsboro and Waco. The Nite Owl in the town of West was a great club. Likewise the Scenic Wonderland in Waco was a huge club where Bob Wills sometimes played. Even when there was no band, you could learn a lot of music in nightclubs. I'd put a nickel in the jukebox and listen closely to learn the words and the chords of songs by Lefty Frizzell, Ernest Tubb, or Hank Williams.

Zeke became a fan of my music, and we became lifelong pals. We raised a lot of hell together, and there were plenty of times that he got me out of some kind of mess. I played gigs mostly on weekends, and I'd always run out of money during the week. So I'd hock my guitar at a pawn shop in Waco. When the next weekend's gigs rolled around, Zeke would help me get it out of hock. I pawned my guitar so often that the guy in the pawn shop played my guitar better than me!

Zeke wasn't afraid to run a hustle when one was needed. One time, he was the night manager of a truck stop south of Hillsboro. It was two in the morning, and there was only one couple in the place. Zeke was sitting on a stool, and he thought, *I'll fall off this stool and pretend to hurt my back. That couple will be the witnesses, and I'll collect the insurance money.*

So he fell off the stool, but the couple didn't see him fall. So he got back on the stool and fell off again. This time he actually hurt his back and really needed the insurance money.

Besides being good at dominoes and bad at insurance fraud, Zeke was really funny. The two of us used to trim trees together for a company in Waco. We were always late to work, and we would give one excuse, then another. Zeke told them his grandmother had died three times!

Later on, we had a weekly poker game in Zeke's trailer house in Hillsboro. All the hustlers in Hill County played. It was me, Zeke, Steve Gilcrease (my poker buddy to this day), and a World Word II vet named Albert, who remained a terrific poker player till he was ninety years old. If you wanted to go home with your shirt, you needed to be a good player.

Rounding out the regular winners was another Texas hustler, Carl Cornelius. Carl was always pulling some kind of shenanigan. Years later, he bought a truck stop on Interstate 35, incorporated a town there called Carl's Corner, and voted himself the mayor. I was driving down I-35 when I saw this huge billboard that said, "Carl's Corner Truck Stop and Restaurant." And it had a big picture of Zeke with me and Carl. I thought, *Well, old Zeke did it again.*

Carl's Corner is right down the road from Abbott, where I still own a home. We were playing poker at Carl's one night, and the game got bigger and bigger, and the next thing I knew, I'd won the truck stop from Carl. The next day, a buddy said, "What are you gonna do with it?" And I said, "Try to lose it back as fast as I can."

Instead of losing it back, I built a concert hall, and a lot of great performers played there. We did one of my Fourth of July picnics there as well. I never made a dollar, but I had a lot of fun. Like I said before, you can't make more old friends.

Booger Red eventually grew up to be Willie Nelson, then Shotgun Willie, the Red Headed Stranger, and a few less-complimentary names I've been called along the way. But it all started in Abbott, and after eighty-plus years, the adventures continue.

Like I said, you can never have too many friends. Even if you do win the lottery.

Dear Zeke,

How is it there in domino heaven? If you can take a break from winning the angels' wings, I'm wondering if there are any good jokes up there? Here's one you might try on the halo crowd:

Three guys are caught in a flood. They climb on a roof and all pray for God to save them. A boat comes along and one of the guys jumps to safety in the boat. The waters are getting higher, and the other two are praying again, when another boat comes and the second guy jumps in. "There's room for one more," he yells. But the third guy waves them away and says, "God will provide."

As the waters rise higher, a helicopter comes over and lowers a ladder, but he waves them off, too, and says, "God will provide." But then the waters come over the house, and he drowns.

The guy arrives at the Pearly Gates. He sees God and calls out, "Oh Lord, why did you forsake me?"

And God says, "I sent two boats and a helicopter!"

That's a good one. I hope for all our sakes that God has a sense of humor.

Sending love from Texas, the next best place to heaven,

Willie

BOOGER RED GETS GOING

When you listen to me braggin' about my home state, you might think I was reluctant to ever leave it. But the truth is, I was always eager to wander. I'd hop a freight train to see where it'd take me. If it didn't go far, I'd hop another to take me back home.

One of my bigger travel misadventures started after a tree-trimming job with Zeke in Tyler, Texas. My job was on the ground, but one of the trimmers needed a rope, so I climbed up to give it to him. Next thing I knew, I fell forty feet from a tree and hit the ground hard. I looked up at Zeke, who probably thought I was dead, and said, "I don't believe trees is my line of work."

That tree company had been paying me eighty cents an hour. The funny thing is, years later, the same company paid me $100,000 to play a concert for them. So I guess it all worked out.

After high school, I was classified 1-A for the draft and soon joined the Air Force, which was willing to take me and my injured back from the tree fall. At basic training, they sheared my shaggy hair like a sheep, and I figured I'd soon be off to the Korean War.

They shipped me first to Biloxi, Mississippi, where I was assigned the important duty of moving heavy boxes. That brought back my back injury and landed me in the hospital for a couple of months. Finally, the Air Force gave me a choice—back surgery or a discharge. Believe me, there was no way I was letting them operate on my back. So nine months after I enlisted, I was discharged and sent home to Abbott.

Soon I had a new band and was madly in love with the prettiest girl I'd ever seen, Martha Jewel Matthews. We soon married. I was nineteen, and she was sixteen. We were both a little spoiled and used to getting our way. I played music in rowdy nightclubs, and she was a waitress. We were both hotheaded and prone to jealousy. What could go wrong?

To add fuel to the fire, Martha was a Cherokee Indian, and I was part Indian on my mother's side and part cowboy on my stubborn side. Me and Martha had plenty of nights of the cowboys versus the Indians, but we had a lot of good times too. We'd have had fewer problems if we'd learned the most important rule of marriage, which is to listen to each other. In marriage and in life, listening to the other person and giving an honest response is key. They may not like what they hear, but at least you're not both living a lie.

The good times were exciting for both of us. I was playing music and working as a radio disc jockey in Hillsboro, then San Antonio, and then Fort Worth at a great station, KCNC.

Every DJ needed a good sign-on, and I started every broadcast with, "This here is your old cotton-picking, snuff-dipping, tobacco-chewing, stump-jumping, gravy-sopping, coffeepot-dodging, dumpling-eating, frog-gigging hillbilly from Hill County, Willie Nelson."

Fort Worth was like the Wild West—not just the stockyards and herds of cows that came right through town, but also the wild nightlife on the Jacksboro Highway. When you played a gig, most of the guys in the band were packing heat, and so were most of the audience. I was the front man for a trio that played an all-night joint called Gray's Bar, which had a mostly Mexican and Black audience that loved our blues and jazz sounds, but which also had chicken wire strung across the front of the stage to protect the band from thrown beer bottles.

Clubs at night, then radio by the day. I was a working fool, and I still wasn't earning enough for a family to live on. So we packed it up and wandered to California, then to Oregon, where we had a couple of good years living with my mom. I had a great DJ stint at KVAN in Vancouver, Washington. Those were fun years. One day I signed on by saying, "This is Willie Nelson, serving the greater Dallas–Fort Worth area." We had a bunch of phone calls saying, "Where do you think you are?" But at least I knew they were listening.

I loved being a DJ and getting paid to play the songs I wanted to play and wanted to hear. I also could use my airtime to promote my shows at night. I never got any of that famous 1950s radio payola money to play particular records, but that don't mean I wouldn't have taken it.

Oregon was beautiful, but it wasn't Texas, and we now

had two beautiful girls, first Lana, and then her sister, Susie. So we went back to Fort Worth and moved in with my dad, Ira, and his wife, Lorraine. I tried a lot of jobs. I sold Bibles for a while but switched to encyclopedias because I felt guilty about selling the big, expensive Bibles to families that couldn't afford them.

Encyclopedias were easier. I'd drive around until I saw a swing set in a backyard. That meant they had kids and needed to open a world of knowledge for them. The company I worked for had perfected a sales technique. If a couple said they couldn't afford to buy encyclopedias, I'd say, "You can't afford to *not* buy them." Once I explained that this advanced education system cost less than a pack of cigarettes a day, most of 'em were hooked.

I joined the Metropolitan Baptist Church and was teaching Sunday school there. One day the preacher called me in and said, "Either you quit playing in beer joints or you quit teaching Sunday school." I protested that the churchgoers were listening to me play in those clubs, but the preacher stood his ground. The choice was pretty easy.

"I ain't making no money teaching Sunday school," I said. "And they're paying good for my shows at the Nite Owl. End of story."

Lana and Susie now had a little brother named Billy, and once again I discovered that my income was well short of my outgo.

I had yet to set the world on fire, but I had a fire burning inside me, and I was determined to make it as a songwriter and musician. I gave Houston a shot for a while and was making ends meet by teaching guitar lessons at a music school run by my friend Paul Buskirk. Paul was a jazz guitar master. He'd teach me a lesson, then I'd teach it to all the students. I usually was about a week ahead of them.

I was writing songs all along and felt like I was onto something and getting closer every day. This was a stretch of hustling years, where I suddenly wrote a string of songs like "Family Bible," "Night Life," and "Funny How Time Slips Away." Those songs, and a few more that have stood the test of time, would truly launch my career.

DEAR TEXAS,

You and me have been together for a mighty long time. We first teamed up when Doc Sims helped deliver me in Mama and Daddy's house in Abbott. I learned to sing in your churches, in your fields, and in the late-night honky-tonks of small towns. Sons of Texas, like Bob Wills and his Texas Playboys, and Ernest Tubb, with his songs of heartbreak and loss, also helped make me who I am. Wherever I go, I still carry that music with me.

Wherever I go, I feel your rivers flowing through my heart. And when we're apart, I miss your wide-open sky. When we're together, I like to walk in your rain and let your thunder fill my soul. After the rain, I listen to the songs of your mockingbirds, and I sing with them—the music of Texas.

For the past fifty years, no man has ever felt more welcome in his home state than I have in Texas. When fools started disrespecting you by throwing litter along your highways, I got the chance to tell them, "Don't Mess with Texas." And it worked, as the litter on our roadsides gave way once again to fields of blooming bluebonnets.

In Texas, I wrote countless songs and recorded dozens of albums that carried my music far around the world. I've never given up my love of playing to audiences wherever they want to hear my show, but it doesn't take me long to start hankering for home.

When I'm on the road, I think of getting back to my Hill Country home in Luck, Texas. When I'm in Luck, I saddle a horse and take a ride while I wait for your beautiful sunset. Soon the sky grows dark, and the stars shine bright as I sing you a song. It's the least I can do.

Your native son from Hill County,

Willie Nelson

TEXAS

by Willie Nelson

Listen to my song
And if you want to sing along
It's about where I belong
Texas

Sometimes far into the night
And until the morning light
I pray with all my might
To be in Texas

It's where I want to be
The only place for me
Where my spirit can be free
Texas

It's where I want to be
The only place for me
Where my spirit can be free
Texas

Listen to my song
And if you want to sing along
It's about where I belong
Texas

To All the Young Songwriters,

Hello, my young friends. So you want to be a songwriter? Well you're in luck, 'cause I've been writing songs for eighty years or so, and I have a piece of advice I think you should consider: Quit now! Quit while you're ahead!

Just think, you may not have had a single rejection yet. Why subject yourself to the negativity and the lack of faith in your talents? Why struggle for what may be years of rejection, doubts, and depression? Seriously, I've written thousands of songs, and I'm here to tell you, it don't get any easier.

So now that you've considered all that, let me ask you square: Are you still writing? 'Cause if you quit that easy, you didn't deserve your talent in the first place. But if you're still with me, read on . . .

For starters, if you want to be a songwriter, listen to the world around you. Listen to the sounds and the thoughts that are passing through you. If it feels right and true to you, it likely will for others. Music is the great communicator. It crosses all boundaries. There is zero difference between people in Texas and people in Japan. We all laugh at the same kind of things. We all cry at the same things. And we all have music wired into our DNA.

It also might be wise to write as many songs as you can. They won't all be good ones, but you gotta start somewhere, and that'll improve your odds.

The great Mae Axton, who cowrote "Heartbreak Hotel" for Elvis Presley, was one of the first stars of country music who saw talent in me and encouraged me to give it my all. One thing she said that I never forgot is that songwriting is serious business. So now I'm telling you, if you want to be a songwriter, you need to give it your all.

Everything in life holds the promise of inspiration. I've done some of my best writing just driving down the highway with a mind that's open for a melody or even just a phrase. Songs don't have to be complicated. Maybe one reason I can still remember those songs I wrote when I was ten years old is because I somehow knew to follow what would become a frequent refrain: "Keep it simple, stupid." You don't need thirty average verses—you need three great ones.

One of my dear friends was the legendary Nashville songwriter Harlan Howard, who wrote classics like "I Fall to Pieces," "I've Got a Tiger by the Tail," and "Heartaches by the Number." I still love my recording with Ray Charles of Harlan's classic, "Busted."

Harlan wrote a thousand songs or more, and his motto was "Three chords and the truth." If you can remember that, and maybe come up with a line or two that memorable, you may be in bidness.

But don't think "the truth" is limited to your truths or that you have to only write what you know. Maybe it's better to write what you know plus what you see, what you hear, and what just comes to you. Whatever it is, write it down.

I don't exactly know where my songs come from, but I'm pretty sure they fall from the sky. Recognizing that, I've become adept at catching them. And knowing that they come from some part of my experience, my longing, my joy, my grief, or something even closer to my core, I've learned to trust them. If a new song strips me bare, I have to be willing to show that part of me to one and all.

Songs come to me in my dreams, and sometimes in my daydreams. Searching for a song, I might look at a situation or a place and imagine myself as some person with a story to tell. That can help me find a song that strikes people as being real.

The songs may come to me rough-formed, but with a beginning, a middle, and an end. Then my abilities as a musician take over, finding the song that I'm hearing and moving things around a little to find the right progressions and tune up the lyrics. I used to think there was no need to even write it down. If I couldn't remember it, maybe it wasn't memorable. But then I got a little older and started thinking, *Write it down and sort out the memorable part later.*

This is "Songwriter," and it's straight to the point.

Write it down what you found out songwriter
Don't let it all slip away
Speak your mind all the time songwriter
Someone is listening today
Write on songwriter
Write on songwriter
Write on . . .

Not long after receiving the creative blessing of Mae Axton, I wrote some of the greatest songs of my life in just a matter of days: "Night Life," "Funny How Time Slips Away," "Mr. Record Man," "Crazy," "I Gotta Get Drunk," and "The Party's Over."

So that's my story. What's yours?

Hope to hear you on the radio,

THE SONGWRITERS

by Willie Nelson

We get to break out of prison
Make love to our best friend's wife
Have a beer for breakfast in Boston
Drink rum in Jamaica that night

We get to tell all our secrets
In a code no one understands
We get to shoot all the bad guys
But never get blood on our hands

We're heroes, we're schemers
We're drunks and we're dreamers
We're lovers and sometimes we're fighters
We're students, we're teachers
We're the devil, we're preachers
We're true love but mostly one nighters
We're the songwriters

Half the world thinks we're crazy
The other half wants to be us
And they're jealous because we get to hang out
In the back of some big star's tour bus

We're old boots and tee shirts and blue jeans
We're cables and strings and E chords
We only dress up in November
When they hand out some writers awards

We're heroes, we're schemers
We're drunks and we're dreamers
We're lovers and sometimes we're fighters
We're the truth, we're the lies
We're stupid, we're wise
We're true love but mostly one nighters
We're the songwriters

We ride bridges, we cross 'em and burn 'em
Teach lessons but don't bother to learn 'em
Our mamas don't know what we're doing
Why we stay out all night long
I told mine I was a drug dealer
She said thank God you ain't writin' songs

We're heroes, we're schemers
We're drunks and we're dreamers
We're lovers and sometimes we're fighters
We're the truth, we're the lies
We're stupid, we're wise
We're true love but mostly one nighters
We're the songwriters
We're the songwriters

WILLIE NELSON

Dear Music Executive,

I already wrote you two letters. One was a note of appreciation to the record man who put a sad song on a jukebox, and one was to the kind of music executives who make creative decisions for artists they're paying to make their own creative decisions.

The first letter, a song I wrote and recorded in 1962, was addressed to "Mr. Record Man." It was a classic Nashville country song, the words of a man with a broken heart. As I've always said, it's the sad songs that make the jukebox play.

Mister record man I'm looking for a song I heard today
There was someone blue singing 'bout
someone who went away
Just like me his heart was yearning
for a love that used to be
It's a lonely song about a lonely man
like me

We sold some records with that one, but the rest of that decade in Nashville didn't do much for my opinion of certain types of record executives. I made a couple of labels some good money, only to get dropped. I could've gotten mad, but I knew that the only thing bean counters respect is beans.

And that reminds me that it's time for a joke.

A musician is in the recording studio and he don't

49

like all the notes and suggestions, so he throws up his hands and says, "All record executives are assholes."

From the back of the studio, a voice calls out, "That's insulting! You can't say that to me!" The musician says, "Are you a record executive?" And the guy says, "No, I'm an asshole."

In the early '80s, when my pal Kris Kristofferson and I were making the movie *Songwriter*, I felt like it was time to write another letter to all the record executives who only see music as a bottom-line endeavor, with their bottom line being the main endeavor.

So Mr. Music Executive, not only did I write you a letter and put it in a movie for you, just to be sure you heard me, I recorded it and sent you a copy, COD, in care of every radio station in America. In case you didn't get your copy, the lyrics are below.

You know who you are. Get your shit together.

Willie Nelson

P.S. Having pointed out the asshats, I should mention there are also a lot of great record men and women out there. After a string of Nashville execs and producers who thought they could improve my sound, I went to Atlantic, where Jerry Wexler was one of the first who treated me square and allowed me to make the records I wanted to make. Those records topped the charts and gave me more freedom. But if you're a record exec today who's treating lesser-known musicians the way I used to feel, please read these lyrics twice. Just like this big old world, we're all in this music together.

WRITE YOUR OWN SONGS

by Willie Nelson

You're callin' us heathens with zero respect for the law
But we're only songwriters just writing
our songs and that's all
We write what we live
and we live what we write—is that wrong?
If you think it is, Mr. Music Executive,
Why don't you write your own songs?

An' don't listen to mine, they might run you crazy
They might make you dwell on your
feelings a moment too long
We're making you rich and you're already lazy
So just lay on your ass and get richer or write your own songs

Mr. Purified Country don't you know
what the whole thing's about?
Is your head up your ass so far that you can't pull it out?
The world's getting smaller and everyone in it belongs
And if you can't see that Mr. Purified Country
Why don't you just write your own songs?

And don't listen to mine, they might run you crazy
They might make you dwell on your
feelings a moment too long
We're making you rich and you're already lazy
So just lay on your ass and get richer or write your own songs

THE HUNGRY YEARS

To give you an idea what my "hungry years" were like, I sold my songs "Family Bible" and "Night Life"—lock, stock, and writing credits—for $50 and $150, respectively. That may not seem right, but we needed the money, and I never regretted it. The enthusiasm for those songs gave me confidence that I really could make it as a songwriter, so I soon climbed into my beat-up Buick and drove to Nashville. I think the car died right before the Nashville city limits.

I rented a rundown trailer in a rundown trailer park, and my family soon joined me. There was real pressure to earn some money, and Hank Cochran ended up being my life-saver. Hank heard a few of my songs and took me to Pamper Music publishing company, where he had a songwriting contract. They didn't have the money to hire me, so Hank gave up his fifty-dollar-a-week raise that was due to him, and Pamper gave that salary to me. I practically jumped for joy. I was a professional songwriter, and my family wasn't broke.

Hank and I started writing together every day, turning out good songs, but still looking for a hit. Our office was in a garage apartment, and we didn't have a phone back there. One day they told Hank he had a call, and he went to the front house to answer it. After he left, I was there alone, looking around, and said, "Hello, walls." Then I said, "Hello, ceiling."

By the time Hank came back from his phone call, I'd

already finished the song. I said I wasn't sure about it, but I sang "Hello Walls" for him, and he said I had a hit.

Faron Young was a singing cowboy—he'd started out making movies, then transitioned to being a Nashville star. Faron loved "Hello Walls," and I offered to sell it to him for $500. He said I was crazy and instead loaned me $500. Then he recorded the song, which went to number one on the charts. My first royalty check was $25,000! I went and found him and gave him a big, wet kiss and tried to pay him back the five hundred.

Faron wouldn't take the money. "You fatten up a calf for me," he told me, "and I'll take that instead." A lot of years later, there was a rodeo in Austin, and they had a champion bull up for auction. My son Billy bought the top bull for $20,000. (I suspect he was drinking at the time.) I had to pay for it, of course, so I sent the bull to Faron and said, "Here's that calf. He got pretty big."

It was a great joke, but Faron used the bull to breed a whole herd of cows, so I guess we all came out okay. And I got a story out of the deal.

Me and the family got out of that crummy trailer pretty fast, but we still weren't on Easy Street. After Patsy Cline rocked the country music world with my song "Crazy," and after "Hello Walls," royalty checks started coming in, but my outflow was still not far behind my inflow.

I went on tour, playing bass with Ray Price's band, The Cherokee Cowboys, and I'd rent the biggest suite at every hotel we stayed in and throw a party for the boys. And I do mean a party. Cheating songs were always popular in Nashville, and I soon learned why. Martha's and my marriage was taking on water from both sides, and it pretty much sunk when I met a singer named Shirley Collie.

Shirley was a great singer, with a yodel that brought crowds to their feet. We ended up settling down on a farm I bought in Ridgetop, Tennessee. I was giving up life on the road for life as a pig farmer. My family all joined me there—Sister Bobbie and her kids too. It was a beautiful time. And I didn't have to worry about going on the road and coming home owing the record company more than I started with.

These were interesting times. My daughter Lana lived nearby. Her husband was a mess, and one day he got physical with her, and I had to go to their house and slap him around and warn him to never lay hands on her again. I was barely back to Ridgetop when he drove by and starting shooting at the house with a .22 rifle. I managed to get one shot off and scare him away, but I had a feeling he wasn't done yet. The next time he came by, I was waiting and shot out his tire. The cops came, and I told them he must have run over a bullet. They wrote that down and were probably glad to get away from our hillbilly feud.

I'd been writing songs in Nashville most of a decade but never really fit into Nashville's idea of a country singer. My songs had too many chords, and I phrased differently than other singers. I knew that, but I only wanted to sing a song the way it sounded best to me. A Nashville producer adding a bunch of strings and background singers still didn't make me into what they wanted.

Just before Christmas in 1969, me and Hank Cochran were writing songs at my house at Ridgetop. We wrote seven songs in one night. The last one was called "What Can You Do to Me Now?"

The next day, my house burned down.

I was at a party in town when Bobbie's son Freddy called me and said, "Uncle Willie, come home fast. Your house is on fire."

I asked him if the garage had caught fire yet, and he said no. So I told him to pull my old car in there. I figured I might as well get the insurance on it.

I raced home, and the fire department was already there. The house was ablaze. The firemen said it was a total loss, and no one should try to go inside. I had another idea and dashed into the burning house. There was a pound of good pot in there. Plus, a year earlier, I'd bought a new guitar that felt like it was made for me. And I didn't want insurance money for it. I wanted that guitar.

Dear Trigger,

I knew you were a classical guitar (a Martin N-20 built in Nazareth, Pennsylvania), and I knew that, with you not having a pick guard, I'd wear your beautiful wood finish down till we both got old and began to look like each other. We're a little beat up, but I think you and me are destined to last the same amount of time. We both know our purpose in this world—to play and be played, though I'm not sure which of us is doing which. Sometimes it feels like you're playing for the both of us.

Your Sitka wood face came from the great Northwest. Your rosewood sides came from Brazil, your mahogany neck from the Amazon rainforest, and your ebony fret board and bridge came all the way from Africa. You were an exotic creature, and I was a hillbilly from Abbott. When you first spoke to me in Shot Jackson's guitar shop in Nashville, I was about shot myself and had given up touring for farming. But when Shot put my old Baldwin pickup in you, what I heard from you, Trigger, was a human sound, the perfect complement to my own voice. And I knew the moment our voices harmonized that we were a match made in heaven (or in Nazareth, I suppose).

I'd loved Roy Rogers, the King of the Cowboys, since I was a boy. And I loved Roy's partnership with his golden palomino, Trigger. Somehow that name seemed perfect for you. You were my horse called Music, and I knew we could ride far.

How much did I love you? When I ran into that burning house to rescue you, people said it was the dumbest thing I ever did, but I knew it was the smartest.

When I look at you, I think of Django Reinhardt, who lived through a fire that crippled his hands but learned once again to become a true maestro of the guitar. I look at you and hear the two of us playing his masterpiece solo, "Nuages."

Fifty years and fifteen thousand shows since we first laid eyes on each other, you are now one of my oldest friends. Tell me truly, "Ain't It Funny How Time Slips Away?" I wrote that one before we met, but the song found its destiny from a dissonant first chord through your every note flowing in unison with my voice, and through our solo that I can hear even in my dreams. Just like "Funny," I've had to live without companions I once loved, but I don't think my music would be the same without you.

So whaddaya say, pal? Want to go for a ride? People are waiting. Let's play.

Willie

FUNNY HOW TIME SLIPS AWAY

by Willie Nelson

Well, hello there
My, it's been a long, long time
How am I doing?
Oh, I guess that I'm doing fine
It's been so long now
But it seems now, that it was only yesterday
Gee, ain't it funny how time slips away?

How's your new love?
I hope that he's doing fine
I heard you told him
That you'd love him till the end of time
Now, that's the same thing that you told me
Seems like just the other day
Gee, ain't it funny how time slips away?

I gotta go now
I guess I'll see you around
Don't know when though
Never know when I'll be back in town
But remember, what I tell you
In time you're gonna pay
And it's surprising how time slips away . . .

Dear Pocket,

What the hell is wrong with you? We've been together a long time, you and me, and it seems like the hole most pockets have at the top is not enough for you and me. You've always had a second hole at the bottom, and sometimes it seems bigger than the one at the top. We should at least let the money stay in you long enough to warm up a bit before it moves on.

But I've got to hand it to you, Pocket, for you and me have our own special arrangement. When I was ten years old and was offered a job playing in a band in a beer joint, Mama Nelson didn't think the nightlife was the right life for a young man steeped in the Lord's music. But when I got home and pulled eight dollars out of you, young Pocket, her attitude changed, for she knew we needed whatever we could bring home.

Me and you sung the empty pocket blues plenty of times. It was a long time before I had a pocket full of real money, but we made up for it with pockets full of dreams. While the dreams were panning out, my pal Zeke was teaching me to play poker in the Zeke style, which meant sometimes having the guts to bet money that we both knew wasn't in my pocket.

The years went by, and eventually I pulled a pencil out of you, Mr. Pocket, and wrote a song called "Crazy." I played my recording of it for Patsy Cline's husband, Charlie, and he took us straight to their house to wake up Patsy at one in the morning to hear it. Patsy recorded "Crazy," and the rest is history. When that money filled you up, we bought a house for my family. But I also went on tour, where I lived the high life that made that second hole in the bottom of you even bigger. Apparently, Mr. Pocket, you and I never heard of a rainy day.

I like Hank Williams's song "My Bucket's Got a Hole in It." In my case, you could substitute the word *pocket* for *bucket* and be closer to the truth. Wynton Marsalis and I recorded "Bucket" for our album *Two Men with the Blues*. The way I see it, if you come from Abbott, Texas, and you're recording Hank Williams songs with jazz masters like Wynton Marsalis, you've got no real beef with where the money goes.

My longtime stage manager, Poodie, used to say, "Willie's got no respect for money. That's why his bills are wadded up." But I figure that if you wad up your money, it doesn't fall out of you nearly so fast. It also takes longer to flatten it out to give it away.

I turned into a pretty good poker player. Lord knows I've had enough experience. But these days, rather than betting money that's not in my pocket, I might win a big hand from a friend who now has to leave the game. I've got his cash, but what good is it gonna do in you, Pocket? It's better to loan or give it back to my friend and keep the game going. After all, I wouldn't want anybody to hock their guitar on my account.

So I guess you and me, Pocket, are doing just fine after all.

Yours truly,

The Man with the Big Hand

NIGHT LIFE

by Willie Nelson

When the evenin' sun goes down
You will find me hangin' 'round
Oh, the night life, it ain't no good life
But it's my life

Many people just like me
Dreamin' of old used-to-be's
Oh, the night life, it ain't no good life
Ah, but it's my life

Listen to the blues that they're playin'
Listen to what the blues are sayin'

Life is just another scene
In this old world of broken dreams
Oh, the night life, it ain't no good life
But it's my life

Oh, the night life ain't no good life
Oh, but it's my life
Yeah, it's my life

THE RED HEADED STRANGER

We rebuilt the burned house at Ridgetop, but I still didn't fit into Nashville's idea of country music. I didn't give up on country music because I believed in what I was doing. I loved Nashville and had a ton of friends there. But to make a living doing shows, I had to be where audiences would pay to see me. And the place where I could always get booked and draw a crowd was Texas.

After years in Nashville, I finally was offered a dream spot to start as a regular on the Grand Ole Opry. The problem was, it didn't pay enough to support my family. It was like when I had to choose between teaching Sunday school and playing honky-tonks. This time I chose Texas. End of story.

People ask me why I love Texas, and it's not just one thing. It's beautiful from the Gulf Coast to the Panhandle, from the East Texas forests to the desert mountains of Big Bend. The people are friendly, the food is good. But lots of pretty places have good food and nice people. In the long run, the magic of Texas is something you have to feel. Basically, you have to be from here to feel the way we do about this state.

"You can always tell a Texan," they say, "but you can't tell him much."

In the meantime, the Nelson family had grown. There'd also been a change to my marriage status. Life on the road is hard on marriages, and things were already rocky with me and Shirley. I met Connie Koepke at a show in Houston, and we fell for each other. This went on for a while, and I was too slow breaking the news to Shirley back in Nashville. She found out about me and Connie when she opened a bill from a hospital in Houston. I have no idea why I used my home address for a maternity bill. Maybe I was afraid to break the news on my own.

So one marriage ended, and another began with the birth of a beautiful girl we named Paula, in honor of her godfather, Paul English.

Me and Paul had been through a lot together. His brother Oliver was a great guitar player, and years earlier, the two of us had played a Saturday radio show back in Hillsboro. One day, Paul came in to listen. I had him take a cardboard box and play any way he liked. I loved what he did right away, but it took me a while to get him in the band.

Paul eventually gave up a successful life of living outside the law to be my drummer, my road manager, and my money collector. Mostly, he was my great friend. He and his wife, Carlene, moved to Texas with us. As did the rest of my band, for we were a band of brothers—and one sister.

With most of the Ridgetop residents in tow, we moved to Bandera, Texas, occupying a former dude ranch that also had the nine-hole Happy Valley Golf Course. We loved it there, but Sister Bobbie, my pal Ray Benson from the band Asleep at the Wheel, and my golf and music buddy, Coach Darrell Royal, all said I should give Austin a try.

Austin is an incredible place. It's constantly growing and changing, but whenever someone moved here is when they say was the heyday. I think if you ask some of the New Yorkers and Californians who are moving here now, you'd find a couple who'd say, "Austin is great, but not as great as it was a month ago."

In 1971, Austin was a small city with a mix of hippies, rednecks, legislators, lobbyists, and college students. I took a look and soon realized they all had two things in common: they loved good music and having fun.

A new music hall in an old National Guard armory was the hot spot, so in 1972, I booked myself to play Armadillo World Headquarters. They took the bar money, and I took the door. This was a time when rednecks and hippies were famous for not getting along, but we had a big crowd of dope smokers and goat ropers, all dancing and drinking beer and happy as clams. That didn't surprise me. I figured if everyone could get along at Woodstock, we could do it in Austin too.

I talked Waylon Jennings into coming to Austin and sharing a show with me at the 'Dillo. He looked at the cowboy hats and hippie girls and said, "Willie, what have you got me into?" Then we put on one of the best shows of our young lives. It felt really good to find all these new young fans.

Dear Paul,

Dear wild, wonderful, crazy, loving Paul. You always had my back. You came from a rough life, and we were connected the moment we met. I knew someday we'd be together to stay. Where else could I find a friend who came from music and from the street, who could pick a lock and pick up the tempo, either one while packing two pistols?

When fate did the inevitable and put us back together, I found out what it was like for someone to truly have your back. In our scuffling days, that meant guarding against locals who didn't like the way we winked at their girls, taking down angry drunks who didn't know what they were up against, and setting things right when promoters didn't want to pay us what we were owed.

Every time I sang "Me and Paul," with you playing that snare drum behind me, we both knew the stories behind our favorite verse:

And at the airport in Milwaukee
They refused to let us board the plane at all
They said we looked suspicious
But I believe they like to pick on me and Paul

Those pistols came in handy a few times, including when you saved the stage and gear at the Fourth of July picnic by shooting a hole in a tarp full of rainwater that threatened to collapse and drown us all.

I was blessed with a great sister, so I guess you were my brother. When my Paula was born, Connie and I knew who to name her for, and we also knew who her godfather should be.

You once called me the eternal optimist, but you were the one who made my optimism into reality. As the years went by, our tours became more peaceful, but that didn't stop you from packing heat while you sat on that drummer's stool, still watching my back and watching over Bobbie and us all.

You looked after the band—you scheduled them, paid them, listened to their troubles, and helped solve their problems the same way you helped solve mine. And when they screwed up, you weren't afraid to get in someone's face and make sure it didn't happen again. At every show, you walked Sister Bobbie from the bus to her piano. And you walked her back again at the end of the show, as reliable as Old Faithful. For fifty years, you made it possible for me to do the thing I love: give the best show I can to every audience.

Losing you was hard. Who was I without Paul? What would I do without my Devil in a Sleepin' Bag? My repeat-offender, badass, outlaw from the Fort Worth police's Most Unwanted list. My great protector and my best friend.

I remember when we were walking down the street in Hollywood all those years ago and I saw a black cape in the store window and said you should wear that onstage. You said you'd look like the Devil, and I said you already did. You wore that cape for fifty years, keeping time behind me, four-on-the-floor or a shuffle beat on your snare—the most underrated and most appreciated drummer in country-jazz music.

What can I say? When your beautiful Carlene moved on to the other side, I was moved to write a song for the two of you, "I Still Can't Believe You're Gone." All these years later, it means more to me than ever. And so does our song, because we truly were "Me and Paul."

And I still can't believe that you're gone,

Willie

ME AND PAUL

by Willie Nelson

It's been rough and rocky travelin',
But I'm finally standin' upright on the ground.
After takin' several readings,
I'm surprised to find my mind's still fairly sound.
I thought Nashville was the roughest,
But I know I said the same about them all.
We received our education
In the cities of the nation, me and Paul.

Almost busted in Laredo,
But for reasons that I'd rather not disclose,
But if you're stayin' in a motel there and leave,
Just don't leave nothin' in your clothes.
And at the airport in Milwaukee,
They refused to let us board the plane at all,
They said we looked suspicious,
But I believe they like to pick on me and Paul.

And on a package show in Buffalo
With us and Kitty Wells and Charley Pride.
The show was long and we was just sittin' there
And we'd come to play and not just for the ride.
And we drank a lot of whiskey,
So I don't know if we went on that night at all.

But I don't think they even missed us
I guess Buffalo ain't geared for me and Paul.

It's been rough and rocky traveling
But I'm finally standin' upright on the ground.
And after takin' several readings,
I'm surprised to find my mind's still fairly sound.
I thought Nashville was the roughest,
But I know I said the same about them all.
We received our education
In the cities of the nation, me and Paul.

YESTERDAY'S WINE

The time we spent in laid-back Bandera seemed far from Nashville in a lot of ways. Though I still owed RCA Records another country album, I was taking time to ponder life while reading Kahlil Gibran's *The Prophet* and sermons by Reverend Taliaferro. I'd been trying to write hit singles, but in a flush of inspiration, I wrote nine new songs and added some earlier ones, similar to "Family Bible," to tell a story that I felt was timeless.

The result was my album *Yesterday's Wine*, a story that followed my natural thoughts as I contemplated my own mortality in a story of imperfect man.

"Perfect man has visited earth already," introduces the first track. "His voice was heard. The voice of imperfect man must now be made manifest; and I have been selected as the most likely candidate."

From "Where's the Show" and "Let Me Be a Man" to "December Day" and "Yesterday's Wine," with its reflections on life, the album chronicles the story of one man. The album ends with "Goin' Home," as the character watches his own funeral. That may not be the makings of a hit record. I think the execs at RCA called it "some far-out hippie shit," and I didn't much care, because I loved it and still do.

My career was stalled, but I felt like my creative arc was shining bright.

YESTERDAY'S WINE

by Willie Nelson

Miracles appear
In the strangest of places
Fancy meeting you here
The last time I saw you
Was just out of Houston

Sit down let me buy you a beer
Your presence is welcome
With me and my friend here
This is a hangout of mine

We come here quite often
And listen to music
Partaking of yesterday's wine

Yesterday's wine
I'm yesterday's wine
Aging with time
Like yesterday's wine

Yesterday's wine
We're yesterday's wine
Aging with time
Like yesterday's wine

You give the appearance
Of one widely traveled
I'll bet you've seen
Things in your time

So sit down beside me
And tell me your story
If you think
You'll like yesterday's wine

Yesterday's wine
We're yesterday's wine
Aging with time
Like yesterday's wine

A FAMILY BAND

In the '60s, Paul became the backbeat of my band, The Record Men, and he would soon become the backbone of what became my Family Band. Paul's brother Billy English joined us as well. Young Bee Spears started playing bass for me in 1968, but he was from San Antonio, so moving home to Texas from Nashville was good for both of us.

We truly became the Family Band when I signed with Atlantic Records, and Sister Bobbie took the first airplane flight of her life as she flew to New York City to play on my album *Shotgun Willie*. It's amazing to think that Sister Bobbie and I started out together, and we ended up back playing together again and have kept playing together for another fifty years. That's one of those great circles that we got to live long enough to see happen.

The band grew in 1972, when Darrell Royal introduced me to a young Dallas harmonica player named Mickey Raphael. Mickey was good. After he'd played several shows with us, I asked Paul what we were paying him. "Nothing!" Paul told me. So I said, "Double his salary!"

Jody Payne had been playing guitar for Merle Haggard. A few years later, I was lucky to get Grady Martin, a Nashville studio legend who'd played guitar on Patsy Cline's timeless recording of my song "Crazy." There were other great players along the way, but the core Family Band rolled down several million miles of American highways together, recorded more albums than I can name, appeared on television and in movies, and had a blast doing it all.

Like any family, we've lost a few members along the way. Those losses were hard, but families persevere. Kevin Smith, a talented bass player, took over in that role after we lost Bee. No one could fill the Bee Man's shoes, but Kevin brought his own talents, and now he's become family too. We're often joined now by my sons, Lukas and Micah, so I guess we're a growing family after all.

Our shows are a little less wild than the raucous Fourth of July picnics of old, when the ladies in the front row were baring all for the band. We didn't mind those displays of fandom; I figured if the crowd was going to be half-naked, I'd prefer for the naked half to be the women.

These days, our big outdoor shows are more likely to have three or maybe four generations of the same family. In other words, they're just like us. And nothing lifts an old troubadour's heart like looking out at a bunch of young fans. That energy going back and forth between us is what helps keep me going.

Dear Family Band,

You really are family, but you know that. We've spent more time on the road and in the studio together than most families get in a lifetime. We've had more laughs than are legally allowed. We've broken ten thousand laws; or maybe we've just broken the same laws ten thousand times. We've played to millions of people. We went from small nightclubs to concert halls and sports arenas, sometimes on the same weekends. In Amarillo or in Amsterdam, we wanted to give them a good show, and we did exactly that, over and over again. Because that's who we are.

We came for the music, but I also remember the laughs; like me wondering why that audience in Vegas was howling with laughter as I sang "Angel Flying Too Close to the Ground." The answer was behind me—Bee Man wearing angel wings and flying on a wire back and forth above the stage. Poodie's motto, "No bad days," was a constant reminder of how lucky we were to be making music together.

We mostly laughed, but sometimes we cried. That's what families do. What did we learn? The same thing we play and sing every night. The life we love is making music with our friends. Even better when your friends are your family.

Big love from the man in
Honeysuckle Rose,

Dr. Booger Red Willie Hugh Nelson, Esquire

Dear Audience,

I guess I should start this more personally, as in . . .

Dear Lady in the Front Row,

Wow! What a view we both had back in the '70s! Sometimes the band told me they enjoyed your show as much as they did mine, so I guess we all were putting on the best show we could. But this letter is not just to you—it's to the whole audience, and to all the audiences. You know who you are. And I want you to know I love you.

Dear Audience, we're all in this together. None of it happens without you. There's no going "On the Road Again" and no singing "Whiskey River" to shouts and cheers unless you're there, waiting for me to get off the bus and on the stage. Those lyrics to "On the Road Again" aren't just a jingle. I really do love my life of making music with my friends. When I've been home a little too long and start saying hello to the walls, everyone knows I can't wait to get back on the road.

When I come onstage, I want you to be happy about it. I kick off the show with "Whiskey River" so we'll all know the party has started. I can't see the faces in the back, but I know you're there, so as I sing those opening verses, I'm looking to catch the eyes of the audience down front. I see you now. And I'm going to sing to you all night.

When you look into my eyes, I want you to see how glad I am to be with you. I want you to listen to my voice and feel my love for music, for my songs, and for you. Our exchange is contagious in all the best ways. As we lift each other up, we lift up those around us. A wave of energy flows out from me to my band and to you. And a wave flows out from you to the crowd around you and reaches farther and farther out, all the way to the back row, then back to me.

We're all together now, and there's a straightforward bargain between us. You've paid to hear me play, and it's my job to entertain you, to make you happy about having bought that ticket. When I sing, "Who'll Buy My Memories?" I'm singing right to you and hoping you'll turn my songs into memories of your own. We call it the Family Band, but the truth is, even though I don't know your names, you're my family too. You're all the girls I've loved before. We're all a Band of Brothers.

So, dear Audience, in the form of that lady in the front row, think of this as my mash note to the girl at the school desk in front of me. I can't dip your pigtails in an inkwell, but I love you yesterday, today, and tomorrow.

I love that my songs have meaning for you, often a personal meaning that touches you deeply. When I sing "Angel Flying Too Close to the Ground," I can feel your connections to the song. And I trust that you can feel me too.

One thing I've learned from a life in music is that if you love someone, you'd better say it while they can hear you. So let me say it now: I love the way you've stood by me through the years, the way you've stood through the rain and through the cold and through the burning Texas sun at my Fourth of July picnics. I love the way you welcomed us to every city, town, and hamlet, to every stadium, concert hall, and two-bit juke joint in America and the world. And I plan on seeing you all soon.

You know where to find me. When I come onstage, I'll be happy to see your smiling faces. I'm gonna give you a wave, a wink, and a smile. Then I'm gonna pick up my guitar, step to the microphone, and start my show the way I always do, with a few sharp strums on the strings and the words that lead to "You're all I got, take care of me."

ANGEL FLYING TOO CLOSE TO THE GROUND

by Willie Nelson

If you had not have fallen
Then I would not have found you
Angel flying too close to the ground
And I patched up your broken wing
and hung around a while
Trying to keep your spirits up and your fever down

I knew someday that you would fly away
For love's the greatest healer to be found
So leave me if you need to, I will still remember
Angel flying too close to the ground

Fly on, fly on past the speed of sound
I'd rather see you up than see you down
So leave me if you need to, I will still remember
Angel flying too close to the ground

So leave me if you need to, I will still remember
Angel flying too close to the ground

SHOTGUN WILLIE

They say to never look a gift horse in the mouth, though that's better than the view from the other end and has less kick. I'd like to add an addendum that you should never underestimate the value of sitting around in your underwear.

In 1971, I was in Nashville at a guitar pull—a late-night session with a bunch of great songwriters showing off their latest stuff. I wasn't sitting around in my underwear—that part comes later—but I had given up on trying to be a Nashville hit machine. Late that night, I played a new cycle of songs I'd written, called *Phases and Stages*. The songs told the story of a husband and wife and the falling apart of their marriage. This was a big step for me. No one had heard these songs, and I didn't know what to expect.

After I finished, a gentleman named Jerry Wexler introduced himself as the head of Atlantic Records, one of the biggest and best in America. Jerry told me they were starting a new country division, and he wanted me to record the album I'd just sung. Knowing a gift horse when I see it, I said, "I've been looking for you for a long time."

Not only did Atlantic want my new music—they also wanted me to use my band and any guests I wanted. We were soon in New York City, recording an album of mostly new material that Atlantic wanted to come out before *Phases and Stages.* As we were laying down good tracks, I was still looking for just the right feel and a title song for the album.

I went back to my hotel one night and opened my mind to let something good come in. It had been a couple of years since that shoot-out with Lana's husband at Ridgetop, but some of the guys were still calling me Shotgun Willie. I was in the hotel bathroom when a phrase popped into my head. "Shotgun Willie sits around in his underwear." I picked up a pen and started writing lyrics on a sanitary napkin package.

Then I got dressed, went back to the studio, and we cut the song "Shotgun Willie," which also became the album name. Atlantic called it my "breakthrough album," and I didn't disagree. After thirty years of working my ass off, I was an overnight success.

You might assume that success changed everything for me, including my attitude. Sure, I had more creative freedom and more cash in my pocket, but I'm not sure it topped the feeling I had when I was just eleven years old and got paid the first time for singing. That was like sitting on top of the world. Remember, I got paid eight dollars one night for playing in John Rejcek's polka band. I'd picked cotton that day for two dollars. Now *that* was a thrill. That first paid performance was the opening of a door on a whole new life. My new albums for Atlantic were just the proof that I'd made the right choice by walking through that door.

SHOTGUN WILLIE

by Willie Nelson

Shotgun Willie sits around in his underwear
Bitin' on a bullet, pullin' out all of his hair
Shotgun Willie's got all of his family there

Well, you can't make a record if you ain't got nothin' to say
You can't make a record if you ain't got nothin' to say
You can't play music if you don't know nothin' to play

Shotgun Willie sits around in his underwear
Bitin' on a bullet, pullin' out all of his hair
Shotgun Willie's got all of his family there

Well, John T. Floores was a-workin' for the Ku Klux Klan
At six-foot-five John T. was a hell of a man
Made a lot of money sellin' sheets on the family plan

Shotgun Willie sits around in his underwear
Bitin' on a bullet, pullin' out all of his hair
Shotgun Willie's got all of his family there

IT'S NOT SUPPOSED TO BE THAT WAY

All the moving around worked fine for me, but it was hard on my kids. Susie was a high school cheerleader in Nashville when we moved her to Travis High in Austin. She didn't see the point in going to a school where she didn't know a soul. I figured she might be blaming me, and I wanted to have a real talk with her, so we went for a drive one day, headed west out of Austin for a loop through the Hill Country. It was a good drive. We ended up in Colorado.

Susie was behind the wheel, and I had my guitar and was writing for my *Phases and Stages* album. I had an idea that one side of the album would tell the story of a divorce from the wife's point of view, and the other side from the husband's, but I didn't have it all yet.

It was hard for me and Susie to talk. I had my guitar and began to write "It's Not Supposed to Be That Way," a song of a father's words to his daughter, words that I found easier to sing than to say. All these years later, I remember singing it to her for the first time as we drove down the highway, father and daughter, crying through their love for each other.

Sometimes it's easier to say what I feel in a song. But either way, I love my kids—every one as much as the next. I also love to sing to them. And I love it when they get up onstage and sing with me. They can sing like angels, and it makes me happy that we sound so good together.

DEAR SUSIE,

This one's for you. Always and forever.

Your Daddy

IT'S NOT SUPPOSED TO BE THAT WAY

by Willie Nelson

It's not supposed to be that way
You're supposed to know that I love you
But it don't matter anyway
If I can't be there to control you

Like the other little children
You're gonna dream a dream or two
But be careful what you're dreamin'
Or soon your dreams'll be dreamin' you

It's not supposed to be that way
You're supposed to know that I love you
But it don't matter anyway
If I can't be there to console you

When you go out to play this evenin'
Play with fireflies till they're gone
Then you rush to meet your lover
And play with real fire till the dawn

But it's not supposed to be that way
You're supposed to know that I love you
But it don't matter anyway
If I can't be there to console you

A LETTER FROM THE ROAD

One thing I've learned. Kids lead to grandkids, and grandkids to great-grandkids. Here's a letter I wrote from the road in 1977, on stationery from the Ramada Snow King Inn in Jackson Hole, Wyoming. My oldest daughter, Lana, had just given birth to my first granddaughter, and I wanted to send her a welcome to this crazy world.

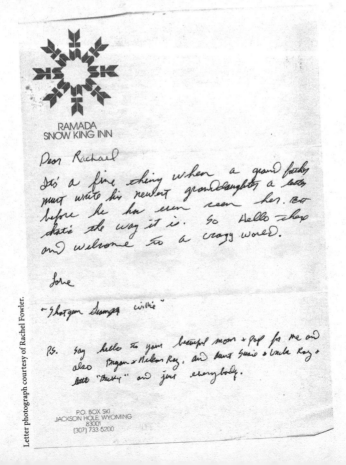

RAMADA
SNOW KING INN

Dear Rachael

It's a fine thing when a grand pappy must write his newest granddaughter a letter before he has even seen her. But thats the way it is. So Hello there and welcome to a crazy world.

Love

"Shotgun Grampa Willie"

P.S. Say hello to your beautiful mom & pop for me and also Greggo & Nelson Ray. and aunt Susie & Uncle Ray & little "Bussy" and just everybody.

P.O. BOX SKI
JACKSON HOLE, WYOMING
83001
(307) 733-5200

Letter photograph courtesy of Rachel Fowler.

MY HEROES HAVE ALWAYS
BEEN COWBOYS

My album *Red Headed Stranger* was the one that finally brought my music to the attention of people all across America. Like *Phases and Stages*, I thought of it as a concept album, with the cycle of songs telling a single story that was greater than each individual track.

Set in the Old West, it's a story of love, devotion, jealousy, revenge, and, ultimately, redemption. In other words, it was a perfect fit for a new kind of country music. The album had triple benefits for me. The record was a hit, but it also got me into movies, and I ended up with my very own Western movie town.

I always loved Westerns. When I was a kid, I'd ride my bike six miles to the town of West and pay a nickel to watch Gene Autry and Roy Rogers on the silver screen. They rode horses and sang and played guitar, and they beat the bad guys. That looked like the life for me. I've always wanted to be a singing cowboy, and that's still the way I think of myself.

"Redheaded Stranger" was an old song that was sung by Arthur "Guitar Boogie" Smith. I had played it on the radio in the '50s, and in the '70s, I would sing the song to my daughters Paula and Amy at bedtime. Sure, it was about a man who shot a lady for trying to steal his horse, but I guess that's my kind of parenting! The song stuck with me, and I fleshed it out with new songs and a few older ones till I had the whole story of a man who murders his wife and her lover, then journeys into the West to seek redemption.

When we made the album, I was planning to make a movie of it and hoped they'd come out at the same time. That didn't quite work out, because it took twelve years to get the movie made. Welcome to Hollywood. The studio big shots wanted Robert Redford to star in the film. We waited, but like so often in Hollywood, nothing happened. So my pal Bill Wittliff wrote a screenplay that had me in the lead role.

While we were waiting on that film, I took a part in Sydney Pollack's *The Electric Horseman*, with Robert Redford. We had some fun, and I got a good lesson in making movies. Wittliff also wrote a beautiful Western called *Barbarosa*, about an old outlaw who is both the scourge and the challenge that drives greatness for a family in their beautiful hacienda in Mexico.

I like making movies and always look forward to a good part. But when someone calls me an actor, I generally say my specialty is more *reacting* than *acting*. Let's face it: no matter the role, I'm still gonna look like Willie Nelson. Luckily, I play myself better than anybody.

We had a public screening of *Red Headed Stranger* last year in the streets of my western town, Luck. It was great seeing the movie in the same spot where it was filmed. Sitting in front of the screen in my Western Town, I felt like I was back in that movie theater in West, Texas.

Like the *Red Headed Stranger* album, the film tells the story of a preacher in the Old West, who loves his beautiful wife and is fully committed to serving God in a wooden church he builds in a small town. One Sunday morning, as the preacher is conducting his Sunday service for the towns-people, a group of drunks gather in front of the church and begin shouting insults to the preacher, the people, and God.

Rather than resort to the violence he's capable of, the preacher addresses the drunks so sternly they are reduced to begging him to stop. While I was writing these letters, it occurred to me that the preacher's curse was a letter all its own.

So here it is. Enjoy.

DEAR LORD,

We're having some trouble here. The Devil's own disciples have gathered at our door.

So what I'm asking, Lord, is that you send a curse down on these heathens—send a visage blacker than night to pluck out their eyes, so they may not see to find this place again.

Send a plague that will turn their lips and tongues to festering rot, so they may never stand here to harp and jeer again.

And if they still persist in their evil mocking, send horrible and eternal death to each man here—and to the seed of his loins—in the form of a thousand generations of crooked vipers. Each viper with a thousand heads. Each head with a thousand fangs dripping with vile poison to strike a thousand times, until there is naught but a weeping and a wailing and great gnashing of the teeth to echo throughout this godless land.

Amen.

The Preacher

DEAR HEATHENS,

You cried that I'd gone too far and begged me to "take that back." Your request is under consideration. In the meantime, I suggest you quit drinking on Sunday morning.

RED HEADED STRANGER

by Edith Lindeman Calisch and Carl Stutz

The red headed stranger from Blue Rock, Montana
rode into town one day
And under his knees was a raging black stallion
and walkin' behind was a bay
The red headed stranger had eyes like the thunder
And his lips they were sad and tight
His little lost love lay asleep on the hillside
and his heart was heavy as night

Don't cross him don't boss him he's wild in his sorrow
he's ridin' and hidin' his pain
Don't fight him don't spite him just wait till tomorrow
maybe he'll ride on again

A yellow-haired lady leaned out of her window
and watched as he passed her way
She drew back in fear at the sight of the stallion
but cast greedy eyes on the bay
But how could she know that this dancing bay pony
meant more to him than life
For this was the horse that his little lost darlin'
had ridden when she was his wife

Don't cross him don't boss him he's wild in his sorrow
he's ridin' and hidin' his pain
Don't fight him don't spite him just wait till tomorrow
maybe he'll ride on again

The yellow-haired lady came down to the tavern
and looked up the stranger there
He bought her a drink and he gave her some money
he just didn't seem to care
She followed him out as he saddled his stallion
and laughed as she grabbed at the bay
He shot her so quick they had no time to warn her
she never heard anyone say

Don't cross him don't boss him he's wild in his sorrow
he's ridin' and hidin' his pain
Don't fight him don't spite him just wait till tomorrow
maybe he'll ride on again

The yellow-haired lady was buried at sunset
the stranger went free of course
For you can't hang a man for killin' a woman
who's tryin' to steal your horse
This is the tale of the red headed stranger
and if he should pass your way
Stay out of the path of the raging black stallion
and don't lay a hand on the bay

Don't cross him don't boss him he's wild in his sorrow
he's ridin' and hidin' his pain
Don't fight him don't spite him just wait till tomorrow
maybe he'll ride on again

— ★ ★ ★ —

BACK IN THE SADDLE AGAIN

When Kris Kristofferson, Waylon Jennings, Johnny Cash, and I were recording our final album as the Highwaymen, Gene Autry came to see us at the studio. All four of us had grown up on Western movies and had since made our share of them. Now that we were all growed up, we looked like a tough bunch of hombres, but as we talked with our childhood hero that day, we all felt like kids.

This was not long after I'd named my son Lukas Autry Nelson, in Gene Autry's honor. While we were all sitting and talking, Johnny Cash said, "Willie, you should ask Gene to sign your guitar." Cash was all heart, and he knew what that would mean to me. Gene held Trigger in his hands and talked about an old Martin guitar he once had. Then he signed my guitar, a treasured and emotional moment that I couldn't have dreamed of as a wide-eyed kid back in that movie theater in West.

It got even better when Gene and all four of us Highwaymen raised our voices and sang "Back in the Saddle Again."

How fortunate I have been.

DEAR GENE AUTRY,

All these years since I watched you on the silver screen, I still get excited when one of your films pops up on late-night TV. Once a hero, always a hero. You were an inspiration to me and to countless others, larger than life and using your persona to encourage goodness in the world. You were a connection to older ways you admired, with an eye to years to come. And it amazes me how well your Cowboy Code holds up as good advice, even today. I still remember it.

GENE AUTRY'S COWBOY CODE

1. The Cowboy must never shoot first, hit a smaller man, or take unfair advantage.
2. He must never go back on his word or a trust confided in him.
3. He must always tell the truth.
4. He must be gentle with children, the elderly, and animals.
5. He must not advocate or possess racially or religiously intolerant ideas.
6. He must help people in distress.
7. He must be a good worker.
8. He must keep himself clean in thought, speech, action, and personal habits.

9. He must respect women, parents, and his nation's laws.
10. The Cowboy is a patriot.

What more can I say? Thanks for leading the way, compadre.

Sincerely,

The Red-Headed Kid
in the Theater Front Row

While I'm reaching out to childhood heroes, I thought I'd toss this one out into the ether.

DEAR WILL ROGERS,

You won't believe the mess we've gotten ourselves into this time. I'm wondering if you can send some advice for our current predicament. I was still a tyke when the airplane you were in bought the farm, but your legend lived on through my childhood, and recordings of your shows were still on the radio. Speaking to me from your place in heaven seemed like a neat trick to a kid in Abbott. Even after you were gone, you were a source of wit and wisdom in the face of the Great Depression and World War II.

That inspires me to think that you may somehow magically receive this letter. Who knows? Maybe you're watching me write it. So I'm sending an update and a summary of a few problems that have us running around like chickens with our heads about to be cut off.

First off, the world is getting hotter. I think you spent enough time outdoors in Oklahoma summers to know that weather hotter than that could lead to all kinds of problems. We know what's causing it, and we've had a good idea on how to stop it for a couple of decades but basically haven't done one goddamn thing. Any advice?

Second, having taken over all the Indian territories, our government has now moved deeply into negative territory.

Our national debt is over $80,000 for every person in America. That's $27 trillion dollars (that's a 27 with 12 zeros and 4 commas after it).

Also, since you lived through the Spanish flu pandemic of 1918, I'm wondering if you have any thoughts on a new virus that is sweeping across the world. Sickness and death would seem to be the biggest threat, but Americans seem more worried about running out of toilet paper. I figgered we can always use the phone book but was reminded that they don't make phone books anymore. Clearly, we ain't getting any smarter.

You also advised to "Never miss a good chance to shut up." So I will take that advice now and hope to receive a reply soon.

Your radio-listening fan,

Booger Red

DEAR BOOGER RED,

This is your radio pal Will Rogers, coming to you via very long-distance waves from my little slice of heaven. I received your recent letter, though I don't know how. I also don't know if you're tuned in to my current frequency, but miracles abound, so here goes.

I'm enjoying my time here and am happy to report that I was right: there are dogs in heaven. That brings me enough joy that I don't think much about worldly matters, but here are a few things I remember once saying that may be of use.

Regarding the temperature: "If you find yourself in a hole, quit digging."

As for the national debt: "Alexander Hamilton started the US Treasury with nothing, and that was the closest our country has ever been to even."

I hope that helps. Remember, things ain't what they used to be. And never were.

Yours from the pastures of heaven,

Will Rogers

HEAVEN AND HELL

by Willie Nelson

Sometimes it's heaven, sometimes it's hell
Sometimes I don't even know
Sometimes I take it as far as I can
Sometimes I don't even go

My front tracks are headin' for a cold water well
My back tracks are covered with snow
Sometimes it's heaven, sometimes it's hell
Sometimes I don't even know

Heaven ain't walking a street paved with gold
Hell ain't a mountain of fire
Heaven is laying in my sweet baby's arms
Hell is when my baby's not there

My front tracks are headin' for a cold water well
My back tracks are covered in snow
Sometimes it's heaven, sometimes it's hell
Sometimes I don't even know

Sometimes it's heaven, sometimes it's hell
Sometimes I don't even know

HIGH ON A HILL

I can't think of a better place to be writing my letters to America than my cypress log cabin that sits high above my ranch, west of Austin. There's an incredible view of the Hill Country in all directions, and big, fenced pastures where my horses live in horse heaven on earth.

I've always loved horses, the beautiful and the not so beautiful. Two of my favorites at Luck were the Dancing Bay Pony, the horse I rode in *Red Headed Stranger*, and a sway-backed old codger named Crummy. I was a terrible calf roper. So one of my smartest hustles was to sponsor a Texas calf-roping competition in San Antonio. Every top rider in the state competed, and the winner roped against me in the finals. That way, I was guaranteed second place. Another Willie hustle!

The number of horses on the ranch has grown over the years. My daughter Amy teamed with me to rescue a herd of seventy beautiful paint horses that were headed to the slaughterhouse. They look a lot better on my hilltop pastures than they would have on some European dinner table. Every time I walk and talk with them, I think, *Okay, score one for the good guys.*

There's plenty of room for Annie and the boys here on the hill. The log cabin's living room has pianos, guitars, and other instruments, so we can play, practice, or write music anytime, night or day. I used to spend a lot of time here on my own. After a day of golf and an evening in the studio, I'd go up to the cabin late and would pass a big rattlesnake that liked to warm himself on my stone sidewalk. I named him Charlie. And me and Charlie, we had an arrangement. I didn't fuck with Charlie, and Charlie didn't fuck with me.

He'd lift his head when I was coming, and I'd sidestep a couple of feet to go around him and say, "Evening, Charlie!" or "Beautiful night, Charlie."

This went on for a long time, and I always looked forward to being greeted by him. But one night, our ranch foreman came to the cabin. I think it was cold, so Charlie had crawled into the space between the screen door and the front door. He was all stacked up in there, and when Bill Polk opened the screen, Charlie came pouring down onto him. Bill whipped out his pistol, and it was goodbye Charlie.

I'd prefer not to kill any of God's creatures but understood what a scare that must have been, so no blame on Bill. Besides, we've got a lot of snakes out here. Some of 'em are driving around in pickup trucks.

Anyway, I'm sitting in what may be my favorite spot on God's green earth and feeling appreciative of the blessings all around me. Tonight, I'll sit on the porch and listen to the coyotes warm up their voices. They're persistent creatures. They've been howling at the moon for thousands of years and are still waiting for the moon to answer.

Dear Luck,

Some say if they didn't have bad luck, they wouldn't have no luck at all. I'm just the opposite. I like to focus on the good luck and let the bad move on down the road. I was lucky to be born where and when I was, lucky to have some God-given talent for music and to have a musical family to help me develop that talent. I've been lucky in love, lucky at the poker table, and I have no doubt that I've been lucky in life.

Some say you make your own luck, and when you see someone who's been lucky, what you often don't see is the hard work they put in. That applies to success in the world of music and on the poker table, where the winners tell stories and the losers yell, "Deal!"

I've never believed in questioning my luck in life, and maybe that's why I named my town Luck, Texas. Not many people are fortunate enough to build a town from scratch, so when my Western movie set evolved into a place where everyone seemed to want to be, Luck was the name that stuck. I like to tell people, "If you're not here, you're out of Luck!"

There's a lot to love about you, Luck. Your Main Street starts at an old chapel where Sister Bobbie and me and the old-time gospel band, The Bells of Joy, have played many an Easter Sunday service. Past the horse corrals is the Luck Opry House, another great spot for live music. And at the far end, where I'm sitting now, is my Luck World Headquarters. What can I say? I like it here. Me and you, we're old friends, and we know each other well. We comfort each other on warm days and cool nights.

I've won and lost a lot of money at this poker table. When this big shutdown is shut out, I'm gonna have all my rowdy friends come over for one hell of a big game. We'll all be in Luck then.

Yours truly,

LADY LUCK

by Willie Nelson and Buddy Cannon

The winners tell jokes
And the losers say deal
Lady Luck rides a stallion tonight

And she smiles at the winners
And she laughs at the losers
And the losers say "that just ain't right"

But they keep right on playing
And paying and praying
Till someday their luck just might change
But if you're surveying at the table and looking for the sucker
Oh by the way sir, what is your name?

Lady Luck rides a stallion tonight
Lady Luck rides a stallion tonight
She smiles at the winners
Laughs at the losers
Lady Luck rides a Stallion tonight

I bet you a hundred, if you still got a hundred
One more wager, winner take all
'Cause sweet Lady Luck likes me a lot more than you
And I'm betting she'll come when I call

Lady Luck rides a Stallion tonight
Lady Luck rides a Stallion tonight
She smiles at the winners
She laughs at the losers
Lady Luck rides a Stallion tonight

When the loser has no more to bet
And the winner's won all he can get
Lady Luck will go riding off in the moonlight
Lady Luck rides a Stallion tonight

Dear Readers,

Good news! We're halfway there, and I'm still writing. If you've gotten this far, then you're still reading, and that makes me happy.

I'm a performer at heart, and these past few months are now the longest I've gone without doing a live show since I was a kid. Even though I still can't do a show and take a chance on my audience members getting sick because of me, I can add a moment of appreciation, just to say thanks for sticking with me. We'll get there yet.

And even if my crowd has to sit separated in family groups, sooner or later, I'm gonna be out there singing. At this point, an audience of one would be an improvement. Speaking of which, where's that dog? I want to play him a song!

One more thing to dislike about this pandammit we're all in: it's a scary enough time that it's hard to joke about it. But that never stopped me. So . . .

A guy goes to the doctor with a lot of symptoms. The doctor runs tests, then sits the guy down.

"Bad news," the doctor tells him. "You have gonorrhea, herpes, and the COVID-19 infection. We're gonna put you in a special isolation room on a diet of flounder, pancakes, and pizza."

"Flounder, pancakes, and pizza?" the guy asks. "Will that cure me?"

"No," says the doctor. "That's the only food we can fit under the door."

If you didn't like that one . . . I'll take your opinion into consideration, 'cause you may be right.

In the meantime, since I am sitting in my own Western movie town, I've decided to write a letter from the Old West to the novel coronavirus. Please read on.

Dear COVID-19,

Fuck you. And as we say in Texas, that goes for the horse you rode in on too. I'm telling you now: this town's not big enough for all of us. And by town, I mean starting with the Main Street of Luck and extending out to include Austin, all of my beloved Texas, and from sea to shining sea of America and beyond into the whole of the world. That definitely includes my adopted home of Hawaii, and all our brothers and sisters, grandparents, and children around the globe.

Let me break it down for you, COVID. Yeah, you got a head start and bushwhacked us when we weren't prepared. Our top elected official didn't want to admit how tough you are, and the next thing we knew, you and your gang of minions had snuck into our saloons, our churches, and every other gathering place, and started sending our loved ones up to Boot Hill.

But that's all over now. This is your high noon. All of us, together, have decided it's time for you to get the hell out of Dodge and every other town. You've been a troublemaker from the beginning, and we have ways of dealing with troublemakers.

We have the greatest army of health-care workers the world has ever known. We have researchers and scientists working for governments and for the private sector, all of them committed to wiping you out the way we did smallpox, a much bigger, meaner, and tougher virus that killed three hundred million people in the twentieth century. That was one badass diablo, but he has been vanquished. There hasn't been a single recorded case of smallpox since 1980. That fucker is no more. And so it will be with you.

While I contemplate your brief obituary, now would be a good time to consider the crucial third element in our showdown. You know what I'm talking about. Just like in *High Noon*, what you fear most is a united community with the courage to act. It took us a while to figure out that you were poorly equipped to slip around town if we all wore masks and kept our proper distance. But now we know your weakness. Now we know what to do. The only question is whether we can all work together to kick your ass.

These are difficult times, but around the world, we've never been more united in facing a common enemy. You've opened our eyes to the reality that our enemies are not other nations or religions we don't unterstand or even other cultures. You're the reminder that manufacturing weapons of mass destruction doesn't guarantee our safety. You're the reminder that money spent on weapons that kill indiscriminately may be money that's needed elsewhere. Walls don't keep us safe either. The way to guarantee our children's safety is to work together until a vaccination and a cure for your scourge is available to people of all lands. Then we can apply those kinds of peaceful solutions to all kinds of challenges.

So my message for you, COVID-19, and for all of your relatives, too, is the same thing I've been saying for much of my adult life. It's something all of us need to say collectively around the world, something we should say to ourselves privately every time we walk into a voting booth. Say it now; say it out loud. Repeat it as often as it takes to truly believe it.

There is a peaceful solution. There really is a peaceful solution.

So fuck off.

Sincerely,

Willie

Sheriff of Luck, Texas

THESE ARE DIFFICULT TIMES

by Willie Nelson

These are difficult times
These are difficult times
Lord, please give me a sign
For these are difficult times

Remember the good times
They're smaller in number and easier to recall
Don't spend too much time on the bad times
Their staggering number will be heavy as lead on your mind

Don't waste a moment unhappy
Invaluable moments, gone with the leakage of time
As we leave on our own separate journeys
Moving west with the sun to a place
buried deep within our minds

And remember the good times
They're smaller in number and easier to recall
Don't spend too much time on the bad times
Their staggering number will be heavy as lead on your mind

Remember the good times
They're smaller in number and easier to recall
Don't spend too much time on the bad times
Their staggering number will be heavy as lead on your mind

BLUE SKIES

I've gotta admit, it feels good to get that "Dear COVID-19" letter off my chest. Writing a book reminds me how smart I was to take typing class in high school. There was one sentence that every typing student in America had to type over and over again: "Now is the time for all good men to come to the aid of their country." Oh yeah, I've still got it!

It's been fun telling you stories of where I came from and how I got to be this recognizable song-singer, Willie Nelson. Now I'm ready to throw a little jazz in the mix. I've always loved jazz, from Hoagy Carmichael and Duke Ellington to Django Reinhardt and Bob Wills and his Texas Playboys, who played their own kind of jazz.

Some people say they don't "get" jazz, but they may be overthinking things. Bluegrass, blues, country, jazz—it's all American roots music, and just like listeners everywhere, it's all connected. After my grandmother taught me that the definition of music is anything that is pleasing to your ear, the rest came natural.

The music business has a need to put labels on music, but a label may restrict the kind of music you create. My guitar hero was the Gypsy jazz guitarist Django Reinhardt. I believe he was the greatest guitar player ever, at least so far. His playing technique, his tone, and his speed were incredible, and listening to him has been a huge influence on me.

I never met Django or heard him play live, but I also was a fan of Frank Sinatra's singing, who of course had great phrasing hisownself. When Frank and I did a show together in Vegas, I told him he'd long been my favorite singer. He told me he loved my singing, which was a tremendous compliment. We became friends, another dream realized, and we recorded a duet of "My Way" for one of his albums.

My interest in those jazz greats and others taught me how to sing and play in the most expressive way. Some people say I sing behind the beat, but I'm in front of it sometimes too. I know where I am, and that's where I want to be.

My bass player Bee used to say my phrasing could lead a band up a creek and drown you, but when I have the right band, I've always trusted that Bee and Paul, or now Kevin and Billy or Micah, will keep the beat and be there for me when I come back to where we started.

After I had chart-topping records with *Shotgun Willie*, *Phases and Stages*, and *Red Headed Stranger*—and a joint record called *The Outlaws* with Waylon Jennings, Tompall Glaser, and Jessi Colter—I was feeling a little pressured to come up with the next big thing. But I wasn't feeling it.

I told my pal Roger Miller I was stuck, and he said, "Willie, sometimes the well goes dry, and you have to wait till it fills up again. That's when you do other people's songs."

My neighbor in Malibu at that time was the great Booker T. Jones, and I asked Booker to produce me singing a collection of pop and jazz standards. The execs at Columbia Records thought I was crazy. They said no one wanted to hear a long-haired, country-outlaw guru sing a bunch of old chestnuts, but I figured the songs were classics, and the record execs were the old chestnuts. Right after that *Stardust* album was released, "Blue Skies" and "All of Me" went to the top of the charts, which may have improved the record company's opinions.

Stardust has since sold six million records, but there's still no point in labeling what kind of music it is. The answer is that *Stardust* is music that people like. There are a lot more great songs I love in the American catalog, so thirty years after *Stardust*, I released my *American Classic* album, with favorites like "Come Rain or Come Shine" and "Baby It's Cold Outside," a duet with my friend Norah Jones.

And I still wasn't done. Three years ago, I released *My Way*, a Frank Sinatra tribute album that won the Grammy for Best Traditional Pop Vocal Album.

We've just finished mixing my second Sinatra tribute album, which will be out in early 2021. The first single is a one-time classic, "Cottage for Sale." After I recorded it, I learned that my old friend Jerry Jeff Walker also was a fan of the song and had recorded it a few years back. We lost Jerry Jeff this past year, but I like to remember him for all the fun times we had together. In the old days, he had a reputation for drinking, and he told me once that the only difference between him and Hank Williams was that Hank went backstage to throw up! Love you, JJ—hope to see you on the next go-round.

Along with those four albums of standards, I've made

and released almost one hundred studio albums, some of them considered gospel, a lot of them called country, some with orchestras, and one recorded in Jamaica with reggae master Toots Hibbert of Toots and the Maytals. I guess the lesson is, I love music, and I love to sing. That's why my goal always has been to be open to making all kinds of great music with people I admire and love. And we don't need no stinking labels!

DECEMBER DAY

by Willie Nelson

This looks like a December day.
This looks like a "time to remember" day.
And I remember the spring, such a sweet tender thing.
And love's summer college,
Where the green leaves of knowledge,
Were waiting to fall with the Fall.

And where September wine,
Numbed the measure of time.
Through the tears of October, now November's over,
And this looks like a December day.

This looks like a December day.
It looks like we've come to the end of the way.
And as my memories race back to love's eager beginning,
Reluctant to play with the thoughts of the ending:
The ending that won't go away.

And as my memories race back to love's eager beginning,
Reluctant to play with the thoughts of the ending:
The ending that won't go away.

And this looks like a December day.

Dear Roger Miller,

Can you hear me, Wild Child? Lemme tell you, these days we could use a few more songs from you, and a little more funny too. All I have to do is think of you, and it makes me smile.

You were like the Lone Ranger and Superman of comedy—quick on the draw with jokes that flew faster than a speeding bullet. Like when that cop pulled you over and said, "Can I see your license?" And you replied, "Can I see your gun?"

Or when your drummer started rushing the beat one night. You turned to him and said, "Play as fast as you want, but we still gotta go till 12:30."

You really lived up to that Wild Child nickname. We did some crazy shit together. At least I think we did. It was the '60s and '70s in Music City, and it's as foggy as it was funny.

I'll never forget riding down the highway with you on a beautiful day. As we gazed at the incredible clouds in the sky, you said, "Just think what God could've done if he had money."

I learned a lot from you. You could be just as fast writing a great song as you were making a joke. You'd finish playing a song during your show, then you'd say, "Here's a song I wrote while I was singing that one." You said you wrote "King of the Road" in ten minutes, and I know how that feels. When the song just comes to you, all at once, you just grab the magic and write it down fast. That's what happened to me with "On the Road Again."

The two of us were one of a kind. We shared a positive outlook on life. If something's wrong and you see the funny part of it, then it doesn't seem so wrong anymore.

You had a gift, but you also knew not to take it too seriously. I'm forever grateful for your advice to sing other people's songs. And I'm pretty sure my record companies are grateful too.

It all paid off for you and me when we recorded our *Old Friends* album at my Pedernales Studios in Austin. We were on fire and having fun. I think we cut the whole album in two or three days and nights. One morning, after an all-night session, we went outside and the sun was coming up. You just squinted and said, "Here comes God with his brights on."

So there you go, Wild Child. You were a one-of-a-kind God's creation, and those angels are lucky to have you.

Give 'em hell in heaven. They could use a laugh too.

I'D HAVE TO BE CRAZY

It's only natural for show-business careers to go up and down. It took me thirty years and fifteen studio albums to become an overnight success, and that was probably a good thing. Sometimes when a young act goes from drawing a hundred to a thousand to a hundred thousand, the temptations to go crazy can be hard to avoid.

We'd also been through years of touring, where you had to be tough not to get hustled or robbed or thrown in jail. Some of my favorite tour and event producers were basically thieves and criminals, but they worked for me, and as long as they didn't steal too much and left enough for me and the band, that was okay because that made them *my* thieves and criminals.

Gino McCoslin was a piece of work who loved to oversell a show. I confronted him once when he sold twice as many tickets as people could fit into the Sportsman's Coliseum in Dallas. Gino just shrugged and said, "Hell, the airlines do it all the time."

One of Gino's favorite tricks was to put a sign on the exit that said "Bathroom." People would go out of the venue by mistake, then he'd charge 'em to get back in. Much of the business was done in cash, and as the band started drawing bigger crowds, the amount of cash got bigger too. My friends Scooter and Bo Franks have been selling my T-shirts since the beginning of time, and that started as an all-cash business.

When you carry lots of cash, you're a target to get robbed. When the band is meeting lots of pretty girls, they prefer to not get accosted by a jealous boyfriend the next time we play the town. There was no shortage of guns on our tour. After a show at Birmingham Coliseum, I heard a gun battle going off right outside the bus. I didn't know what was going on, but I decided to try to keep the peace. When the troublemakers saw me step off the bus wearing cutoffs and tennies, with a pair of Colt .45 revolvers, the problems seemed to melt away.

We were called Outlaws, a term that added considerably to the wild and crazy factor, but we also were playing the long game. We learned the hard way that if our buses stayed in town after the show, the band would party all night and pay the price the next day. So we took a different approach and left the show soon after it was over. By the time the crowd was looking for us to party, we were rolling down the highway.

It also helped that cocaine was banned from our tour. Coke will make you crazy and make you do crazy things, and my rule was, "If you're wired, your fired."

That doesn't mean we didn't have fun. As the crowds got bigger and bigger, we partied more on golf courses than we did in bars. And we partied onstage, pulling out all the stops for tens of thousands of wild and wonderful, dancing Willie Nelson fans. Would I do it all again? Hell, that's the point. I can hardly wait to go do it again.

To All the Girls I've Loved Before,

Now I've got your attention! Am I about to spill the beans in a personal letter that anyone can read? Or am I reminding you that Julio Iglesias and I had a number one, chart-topping, certified-by-precious-metals album and song of that name? The songwriters, Albert Hammond and Hal David, made a little scratch on that. Me and Julio did pretty well ourselves. Sales are always nice, but there was a double bonus because Julio gained a lot of US fans, and I found new fans around the world.

But the first question remains: Is this a letter to all the girls I've loved before, or am I just being appreciative of a beautiful song that God sent my way? Shoot, maybe I'm writing a sequel and hoping God will smile on me again. So here goes . . .

To All the Girls I've Loved,

You remember me, and I remember you. And when I think of you, I smile. We were younger then, and we had our ups and downs—in good ways and bad—but we both seemed to think the way Kris Kristofferson wrote, that the going up was worth the coming down.

But our younger and sexier selves weren't as smart as we thought we were. We're older and wiser now, and as the calendar pages peel away, the hard times fade, and what remains are our smiles and our laughter, and our dancing in the rain. What a time we had, dancing and prancing in the moonlight.

Do you remember when I sang you a love song? That was a song where nothing went wrong, and it's important to remember that nothing really went wrong for any of us. When we let the hard times go, what remains are the good times. When I think of you, it brings me a smile, and I hope the same goes for you.

To all the girls I've loved—you remember me, and I still remember you.

Love,

Willie

LOVE JUST LAUGHED

by Willie Nelson and Buddy Cannon

She said, "Please don't let me go"
I said, "I gotta let you go"
And love just laughed

That's all that I remember
It was a bitter cold December
And love just laughed

Love is still laughing
But you can't go back
What's done is done
Yeah, that's a fact

But it was fun in a strange kind of way
We can look back and smile and say
"Whatever happened brought us down to the day"
That love just laughed

And then love cried
I said, "Where are you going?"
We're just getting started
And love just laughed

We were meant for forever
But that's turned into never
And love just laughed

Love is still laughing
But you can't go back
What's done is done
And that's a fact

But it was fun in a strange kind of way
We can look back and smile and say
"Whatever happened brought us down to the day"
And love just laughed
And then love cried

Love is still laughing
But you can't go back
What's done is done
That's a fact

But it was fun in a strange kind of way
We can look back and smile and say
"Whatever happened brought us down to the day"
Love just laughed
And then love cried
And then love cried

BAD BOYS AND BAD GIRLS

Now that I've come this far and dove in so deep, I might as well get the rest of the nudity material out of the way. So how about a joke?

> A couple is celebrating their sixtieth anniversary, with a special breakfast. The husband says, "I still remember having breakfast naked with you the morning after we were married." And his wife says, "We're not so old—we can do that again."
>
> So they're sitting naked at the table having breakfast, and she says to her husband, "After all these years, you still make my nipples hot."
>
> "I'm not surprised," he tells her. "One is in your coffee, and the other is in your oatmeal."

Ha. And if you didn't think that was funny, wait twenty or thirty years. You'll get it eventually. The important thing to remember is that an onion can make people cry, but there's never been a vegetable that can make people laugh.

Speaking of funny, a few years back, I wanted to make a video of my song, "You Don't Think I'm Funny Anymore." We brought thirty fast Bad Boy lawn mowers to my western town, and we staged a Bad Boy / Bad Girl Lawn Mower Race. In another of my hustles, I bet Owen Wilson and Woody

Harrelson $10,000 that Jessica Simpson could beat them in the race.

We rigged it for Jessica to win, but we also spent the weekend gambling on everything in sight. My favorite part of the video was my longtime roadie Poodie Locke dressed as a woman (with a beard) wearing an "I 'Heart' Owen" T-shirt.

It's important not to take yourself too seriously, and laughter really is the best medicine (though cannabis isn't far behind).

YOU DON'T THINK I'M FUNNY ANYMORE

by Willie Nelson

You don't think I'm funny anymore
You used to laugh at all my jokes
Even though you heard them all before
But you don't think I'm funny anymore

I used to fake a heart attack
and fall down on the floor
But even I don't think that's funny anymore

I guess things change
And the more they change
the more they stay the same
And there ain't no blame
Sometimes the picture just don't fit the frame
And this is where the cowboy yields the floor
'Cause you don't think I'm funny anymore

I guess things change
The more they change
the more they stay the same
There ain't no blame
Sometimes the picture just don't fit the frame

And this is where the cowboy yields the floor
'Cause you don't think I'm funny anymore
Did you hear the one about the dirty whore?
Oh, I forgot, you don't think I'm funny anymore

— ★ ★ ★ —

STRING OF PARS

I got bit by the golf bug after we moved back to Texas. My promoter buddy Larry Trader was also a golf pro, and Larry soon had me and the band playing a lot of golf. We weren't that good, and we liked it that way.

When we made the move to Austin, I bought a rough-and-ready nine-hole course called Pedernales Country Club. It came with a clubhouse—which we turned in to a first-class recording studio—and a bunch of condos that were perfect for my band and any visiting musicians.

We called it Cut-N-Putt. We'd play golf all day and record in the studio all night. I can't remember if we ever slept. The rules on the official scorecard stated, "No more than twelve in your foursome," and "Please leave the course in the condition in which you'd like to be found."

It was a wild game—anywhere from five to fifteen of us playing in one group, each in our own carts, racing to claim one of the balls after the last tee shot was hit. My motto was, "May the fastest car win!" The only thing we stopped for were jokes.

A woman goes to the pro shop and says, "Do you have anything for a bee sting?"

The pro says, "Where did you get stung, ma'am?

She says, "Between the first and second hole."

And the pro says, "Well, first of all, ma'am, your stance is too wide."

If I told one like that, Ray or Turk or Fromholz might have a comeback joke, or they'd double the bet to a million pesos a hole. The next thing you knew, we'd played thirty-six or forty-five holes, and the sun was going down. Songwriter Steve Fromholz was a great music and golf pal and one of the funniest guys ever. "If you drink a big shot of tequila," he told us, "then hold the empty shot glass up to your ear, you can hear a bunch of Mexicans laughing at you."

My buddy Turk used to juggle a driver, a golf ball, and a tee, which was great coordination, but if we got him high, we could still beat him at golf.

Ray Benson, one of my oldest Austin buddies and a legend of Texas swing music, was part of that group. Whenever we made a par, Ray would say, "That's one in a row!"

And my pal Bud Shrake was our golf guru. Bud was a Texas legend. He was a reporter in Dallas the day Kennedy was shot. He'd written about America's greatest sports heroes. And he knew more about the golf swing than all of us put together and was determined to learn the "secret move" that would make every swing perfect. But you also knew that Bud didn't come for golf. He came for the friendship.

Talking about good friends, there was none better than University of Texas football coach Darrell Royal. Coach and I became friends in the '60s, around the time his team at the

University of Texas won the national college football title. He came to hundreds of shows, and it seems like we played a million holes of golf together.

I never was a great golfer, but if I just relaxed and hit the ball the way it felt right to me, I did all right and could hold my own in a match for bragging rights or for $1,000 a hole. One secret for that big bet—make sure you have the right partner.

My partner was usually Larry Trader, who'd done a lot of hustling in his day. Johnny Bush sent Larry to me in the '60s because I was having a hard time collecting what nightclub owners owed me after a show. Trader showed up the first time in a convertible Cadillac and walked into the nightclub office with a violin case. And I can guarantee he didn't have a violin in that case. After that, we never had any trouble getting our money.

Larry and I took on all comers in partners golf. He was my golf pro, but he didn't try to change my swing. Doing things the way someone else tells me to has never worked for me. I like to do things my way. On the road, we used to say, "We're gonna keep doing it wrong till we like it that way."

Focusing on impossible perfection at golf will ultimately drive you nuts. I don't believe my enjoyment of the game or the day or the hole we're playing should be dictated by something as haphazard as a golf swing.

When I head to my home on Maui, the golf game continues at the nine-hole Maui Country Club. It reminds me of Pedernales but is a lot greener. I had a game there with my buddy Jim Fuller, who owned our local restaurant and concert hall, Charley's. Fuller and me played for $100 a hole, and we kept at it for years. He started beating me bad one year, when he was hitting an iron off the tee and never losing a ball. So I gave him one of those new big-headed drivers. He hit it a mile the first time and was hooked. I think I won a couple of thousand bucks from him while he tried to figure out how to hit that driver again. Eventually, he gave up and went back to his way and won his money back.

Golf is a good family game, and playing with my boys, Lukas and Micah, has been a joy. They're both pretty good. When we play Maui Country Club, there's a hole with a tee close to the ocean. Every time we get to that tee, Lukas hops the fence, runs, and jumps into the ocean, then runs back to hit his drive. How can you not love that?

I don't play as much as I used to, but I still like to get out there when the weather is just right and soak in the sun and count my blessings for another day on God's green earth.

DEAR GOLF GODS,

Thanks for not striking me down with lightning. Thanks for all the good company and the good fun. Thanks for my hole-in-one on Maui.

> Speaking of golf gods, do you remember the preacher who decides on Sunday morning that it's too pretty to be stuck in church? He tells the assistant pastor to give the sermon, then drives fifty miles to an empty golf course, where no one will see him.
>
> Jesus looks down on this, then turns to his Father and says, "You gonna let him get away with that?"
>
> God smiles, and as the preacher swings on the first hole, God flicks his finger, and a gust of wind catches the ball and carries it four hundred yards to the green, where it goes in for a hole-in-one.
>
> "Why'd you reward him for bad behavior?" Jesus asks.
>
> God smiles and says, "Who's he gonna tell?"

The joke's on us. And the lesson is, we don't do good things for ourselves or for others to be noticed. We do them to be good.

Your golfing son,

Willie

THIRTY-FIVE YEARS OF FARM AID

When we held the first Farm Aid concert in 1985, I had no idea that thirty-five years later, we'd still be doing our best to support America's family farmers. There were eight million family farmers in America when I was growing up. Eight million! By 1985, that number was down to two million. This wasn't an accident. It was a conspiracy by Big Ag and government to run the little guys out of business. With the help of Neil Young, John Mellencamp, Bob Dylan, B.B. King, and many more great artists, the first Farm Aid concert raised $7 million for family farmers.

Under the stewardship of my friend Carolyn Mugar, we've continued to raise money and awareness at the annual Farm Aid concert, to offer support to family farmers however we can, and to put pressure on people in Washington, DC, to make sure everyone has access to good, healthy food. We've raised $60 million to support America's family farmers, and I sign every check.

I'd like to brag and say we turned the whole thing around, but at best, we've only slowed the decline. That simple truth is hard to see because the big food conglomerates spend big bucks in DC to create policies that benefit them and hurt family farmers and consumers. Because of climate change, farmers now face more unpredictable and dangerous weather than ever. And the mass-produced American diet that comes from the corporate agriculture is literally killing us.

I believe America is better than that. And I do see some positive signs, with more Americans returning to farming. We've helped raise awareness about local and sustainable farming and have been part of a movement toward more farmer's markets where Americans can buy fresh food that's grown by people who care about that food and the land it's grown on.

Congress needs to understand that billions of dollars of support for giant corporate farms ignores the fact that farmers who live on the land are as important to us as health-care workers, police officers, firefighters, and our members of the military. When your average corporate CEO makes nearly three hundred times the average American income, it's time to recognize that something is wrong. And when family farmers struggle to make even that average income, the time for action is long overdue.

Unable to assemble an arena full of music fans during the COVID-19 pandangit, we produced Farm Aid 2020 as an online concert that presented great music and told some compelling stories from America's family farms.

When we announced the concert, I said, "The pandemic has shown everyone that our corporate-dominated food system is fragile and unjust. Now more than ever, it should be clear to all of us how much we need family farmers and why it's so important to listen to them and support efforts—at home, locally and nationally—to keep them on the land."

We raised another million dollars to keep the work going and move us toward a long-term solution. I really hope that every one of you, my readers, will consider where your food comes from and how you can help make America stronger by supporting our family farmers and by voting for office-holders who will work for the good of all.

Dear Family Farmers,

You are the backbone of America. The stock market can make someone rich or bankrupt them, too, but you can't eat stocks and bonds. I grew up in a farm town. Sister Bobbie and I worked in the fields like other families who needed money in the Great Depression. Later on, in Nashville, I tried being a pig farmer, and I know how hard you have to work and how smart you have to be to keep a family farm alive.

I still don't know how you overcome all the challenges. Given a choice, I might play poker till four or five in the morning, the same time you're making a pot of coffee and starting a workday that will likely continue until dark. In the evenings, there's paperwork and planning and trying to figure out how to make the money last from season to season. You've armed yourselves with computers to monitor the weather and crop forecasts; you've harnessed new technology to grow more food with less water and little or no pesticides, and likely every member of your family is a working member of the team.

Factory farms are a sickness and you, our family farmers, are the cure. Speaking for all Americans who care about the food we eat (and that should truly be all Americans), we love our farmers. And we love your dedication to our well-being. We want you to know that we're with you. And that our numbers are growing.

To put a seed in the ground is an act of faith. Keep the faith. And we'll do our best to help you make it so.

Willie Nelson

Cofounder, Farm Aid

HEARTLAND

by Bob Dylan and Willie Nelson

There's a home place under fire tonight in the Heartland
And the bankers are takin' my home and my land from me
There's a big achin' hole in my chest now where my heart was
And a hole in the sky where God used to be

There's a home place under fire tonight in the Heartland
There's a well with water so bitter nobody can drink
Ain't no way to get high and my mouth
is so dry that I can't speak
Don't they know that I'm dyin', Why nobody crying for me?

My American dream
fell apart at the seams.
You tell me what it means,
you tell me what it means.

There's a home place under fire tonight in a Heartland
And bankers are taking the homes and the land away
There's a young boy closing his eyes tonight in a Heartland
Who will wake up a man with some
land and a loan he can't pay

His American dream
fell apart at the seams.
You tell me what it means,
you tell me what it means.

There's a home place under fire
tonight in the Heartland

THE ROAD GOES ON FOREVER

While you're sitting at home, it's natural to think about friends you'd like to see and give a hug. High on my list would be my fellow Highwaymen—Johnny Cash, Waylon Jennings, and Kris Kristofferson. They called us a country supergroup, but mainly we were old friends who loved making music together.

Touring with those guys was the most fun I've ever had with my clothes on. The whole thing started with us going to Switzerland to film a Christmas special. At our first photo session, a reporter asked why we were going to Switzerland to do a Christmas show. And Waylon said, "'Cause that's where the Baby Jesus was born." I knew then we were in for a great time.

Our name came from the Jimmy Webb song "The Highwayman." The song was a perfect fit for the four of us to sing its four verses about a wandering soul who comes back again and again and again, as a highwayman, a sailor, a construction worker on the Hoover Dam, and a captain of a starship.

We'd all known each other for a long time, but we'd also been a bunch of lone wolves, and it was tremendous to be onstage with those guys and our great band. We went around the world together—Europe, Australia, New Zealand, China, Japan.

When we played Tokyo, we all thought, *What does Tokyo know about our music?* But the show was standing-room only, and when we took the stage, we looked out and saw a huge flag out in the audience that said "Tokyo, Texas." And we knew it was gonna be a great night.

From that first song all the way through our third album, where we sang "The Road Goes on Forever," Robert Earl Keen's song about a bank robbery gone wrong, we really felt like highwaymen. But when we toured, it was a family affair. We took our kids and wives with us around the globe. We had 278 pieces of luggage! And I only had one!

I thought it was fun watching Kris and Waylon argue about politics. They argued, but I knew they loved each other too. Like the great Guy Clark song we recorded, we really were "Desperados Waiting for a Train." Me and Kris are in no hurry to board that train, but one of these years or decades, all four of us are gonna be together. You can think of us as really being "Riders in the Sky," but I think we'll just be proving the premise of a beautiful song.

I'd write the guys a letter, but the truth is, "The Highwayman" song was a letter we sang to each other every night. So I'm just gonna sing it one more time for them, while I think about that flag in Tokyo, with Cash closing it out like the voice of God.

THE HIGHWAYMAN

by Jimmy Webb (as sung by Willie, Kris, Waylon, and Cash)

(Willie)
I was a highwayman
Along the coach roads I did ride
With sword and pistol by my side
Many a young maid lost her baubles to my trade
Many a soldier shed his lifeblood on my blade
The bastards hung me in the spring of '25
But I am still alive

(Kris)
I was a sailor
I was born upon the tide
And with the sea I did abide
I sailed a schooner round the Horn to Mexico
I went aloft to furl the mainsail in a blow
And when the yards broke off they said that I got killed
But I am living still

(Waylon)
I was a dam builder
Across the river deep and wide
Where steel and water did collide
A place called Boulder on the wild Colorado

I slipped and fell into the wet concrete below
They buried me in that great tomb that knows no sound
But I am still around
I'll always be around and around
and around and around and around

(Johnny)
I'll fly a starship
Across the universe divide
And when I reach the other side
I'll find a place to rest my spirit if I can
Perhaps I may become a highwayman again
Or I may simply be a single drop of rain
But I will remain
And I'll be back again and again
and again and again and again

WHISKEY RIVER

L et's talk whiskey. Or we can sing whiskey. I'd rather sing about it than drink it. Same thing for cigarettes, 'cause the two of them teamed up to kill me and damn near succeeded.

Someone asked me recently, "What was the smartest thing you ever did?" I didn't even have to think about it. It was quitting cigarettes and whiskey. Then they asked me, "What was the dumbest thing you ever did?" Didn't have to think about that either: cigarettes and whiskey.

When I was young, it seemed like everyone my age smoked and drank. When you start playing music gigs, you think you look cool playing guitar with a cigarette hanging from your lower lip. I've got a photo of Django Reinhardt doing it, and I idolized Django.

It's the easiest thing in the world to start smoking. Same thing for drinking. But it's not so easy to stop. I've seen better guys than me try to quit drinking and fail, and they're all dead. That includes too many people I love. God bless them every one. Same thing with cigarettes. I know how hard it was for me to quit, and I know lots of them tried their best.

If it hadn't been for pot, I'm not sure I'd be alive today. Whiskey and nicotine were my troublemaking pals. A cigarette made me want a drink, and a drink made me want a cigarette. We had some fun together, but I wasn't always a fun drunk. The hangovers definitely weren't fun.

After thirty years, I began to see they weren't such great friends after all. I didn't feel good without them. And I didn't feel good with them. To make it worse, the cigarettes had my lungs and my singing voice all tied up in knots. One year I had four bouts of pneumonia. In 1981, I was running on Maui on a hot day, then I jumped in the ocean, and my lung collapsed. I was lucky to make it back to the beach.

Maybe I was trying to show that I could start all over, but I cut off my long braids and laid them back on my shoulders on my hospital bed. When my manager Mark came to see me, I told him the medicine they gave me had some bad side effects and handed him the braids. He nearly fainted.

I knew then it was time to delete and fast-forward. When I got out of the hospital, I opened up my pack of Chesterfields and threw all twenty cigarettes away. Then I rolled up twenty joints, and a new Willie was born. I've never smoked a cigarette since and haven't sampled much whiskey either. I guess I just don't need them.

Unfortunately, there've been a few officers of the law who didn't think I needed marijuana. I got myself into occasional trouble, but troubles are inevitable, and it's up to us to get ourselves out of hot water. Sometimes you have to get creative. I had to sing "Blue Eyes Crying in the Rain" at the courthouse in Sierra Blanca, Texas. I played golf with my longtime pal Sheriff Jack shortly after getting out of his jail, where I spent a few hours because some deputy thought I'd make him famous. Worst of all, I missed my dear friend Ann Richard's funeral when the bus got pulled over and searched. That one hurt.

But a funny thing happened on the way to the hoosegow. Every time we got busted, something good came out of it. Across our nation, there was more awareness and then resistance to long and unjust jail sentences. Not everyone gets to sing their way out of possessing a few joints.

Over the years, Black Americans have been four times more likely to get busted than their White neighbors. White or Black, those sentences destroy lives and families, and it costs a lot of tax dollars to lock people up for nonviolent crimes. Support grew for legalizing what much of the country was doing already. When the federal government didn't take action, individual states began decriminalization and legalization on their own.

I believe that within a decade, medicinal and recreational marijuana will be legal in all fifty states. We'll have a minimum age limit; youngsters don't need to smoke up their lungs or their brains. But on the high end of the age scale, there'll be no limit, because the aches and pains of age are better addressed with cannabis than painkillers. And the tax revenues will be a boon to all fifty state governments.

I didn't set out to be the unofficial spokesperson for marijuana and sensible marijuana laws. I didn't expect to be called the world's most legendary stoner. Nor did I expect to be the corporate CTO—chief tasting officer—of Willie's

Reserve marijuana and Willie's Remedy CBD products (all of it grown by independent family farmers). But here I am. People ask me which of our products is my favorite, and I say, "It's like sex—they're all good!"

I've bought a lot of pot, and now I'm selling it. But I'm not telling anyone to smoke it. That's each person's choice. For me, it works. I can be a little high-strung. Sometimes I say the reason I smoke pot is so I don't kill someone.

I've been smoking weed so long, I've become the canary in a coal mine to look at its long-term effects. I think it's obvious that any smoke in your lungs is gonna have an impact—not a good thing for a singer with a lot of songs left to sing. That said, I've never known anyone to get killed by pot, but if a bale of it fell on your head, that might be a different story.

One morning not long ago, I woke up and was surprised to read that I'd quit smoking pot. It was pretty funny—people were acting like the world was coming to an end. So let's be clear: I haven't given up marijuana, but I don't smoke a lot of joints like I used to.

Luckily, there are alternatives to smoking, like vaporizers. Plus, my sweet Annie is the queen of edibles. Annie is the boss of Willie's Reserve and Willie's Remedy. I really am the taste tester, and I think it's time for me to get to work. That's all for now. See ya in my dreams.

Dear Cannabis,

What can I say? You saved me, and we both know it. I met you way back in 1954, when a fellow Fort Worth musician asked if I wanted to "blow some tea." I knew he meant marijuana, but I'd heard stories about what you might do to me. So I turned you down, but my pal gave me a slender joint and told me to smoke it sometime. I gave you a try, but I smoked you like a cigarette and didn't hold you in my lungs. It took a few times for me to figure it out, but when I did, I had a feeling we'd eventually be friends.

Lots of folks said we were doing wrong, but I know love when I see it. And I don't believe the seeds and flowers that were given to us from a creator are any more illegal than the hops that are used to make beer or the grapes that make wine.

We've had quite a run, and they like to make jokes about me and you. They say we tour the county in a cannabus!

People say, "When you smoke pot you get high, but when you smoke Willie's pot, you get Willie high!"

An astronaut came on the bus, and we were talking and laughing, and he said I was the only person he'd met that'd been higher than him.

My pals write songs about getting too high with me. Toby Keith sings, "I'll never smoke weed with Willie again." And if we're on the same bill, he might be smoking weed with me again right after the show.

Comedians make jokes about you and short-term memory, but I can't remember any of them. I must be high.

If I let a few thoughts slip from my mind, the good news is that the first ones I let go of are the negative thoughts. As I've always said, "Don't think no negative thoughts."

Cannabis, I suspect you were a little heartbroken when word went around that we broke up. But I think you knew. Just like Annie and me, you and I are a couple to the end.

Sometimes people ask me how much of you I've smoked, but there's no answer. We've been pals so long, we're just smoking each other, getting each other high, and opening ourselves to the possibilities of now. I finally got around to writing a love song about the two of us. I love to sing it, and the audiences love to sing it with me. So everyone, all together: "Roll me up and smoke me when I die!"

High on a hill,

168

ROLL ME UP AND SMOKE ME WHEN I DIE

by Willie Nelson and Buddy Cannon

Roll me up and smoke me when I die
And if anyone don't like it, just look 'em in the eye
I didn't come here, and I ain't leavin'
So don't sit around and cry
Just roll me up and smoke me when I die

Now, you won't see no sad and teary eyes
When I get my wings and it's my time to fly
Call my friends and tell 'em
There's a party, come on by
Now just roll me up and smoke me when I die

Roll me up and smoke me when I die
And if anyone don't like it, just look 'em in the eye
I didn't come here, and I ain't leavin'
So don't sit around and cry
Just roll me up and smoke me when I die

Hey, take me out and build a roaring fire
Roll me in the flames for about an hour
Then take me out and twist me up
And point me towards the sky
And roll me up and smoke me when I die

Roll me up and smoke me when I die
And if anyone don't like it, just look 'em in the eye
I didn't come here, and I ain't leavin'
So don't sit around and cry
Just roll me up and smoke me when I die

HAPPY BIRTHDAY, WOODY!

Hey, pal. Wish I was there to celebrate with you (wherever "there" is). I'm on the hill in Austin, still in quarantine, bored to fucking death and missing playing poker and telling bad jokes. Speaking of which . . .

A couple were doing their thing on the second floor of a whorehouse. They were doing it in the open window, got excited, and fell out onto the street below.

So a drunk bangs on the front door, and when a lady opens it, he says, "Madam, your sign fell down!"

My guess is the sign was still working.

Woodrow, I'm looking forward to being back on Maui and mixing up the dominoes and burning one with you. We've had some good times making movies and television together, and it was fun watching you learn to play golf in Austin. But it was even more fun watching you learn to play dominoes and poker. Most people would have given up after a few of your beatdowns, but you're a pigheaded son of a gun and were determined to get it right or lose trying.

I want to say thanks to you and to Owen Wilson for your generous contributions to the beautiful Woody Harrelson wing on my house on Maui. I know you're determined to win all that money back, and I want to encourage you to drop by anytime to give it a shot. My door is always open to a good friend with a pocket full of hundreds.

You busted me up when you wisecracked that people who wish I were president don't realize that I'm a "fucking hustler." That's about the nicest thing anyone ever said to me.

I think we've burned down a forest of marijuana together since that first joint on the bus in L.A. That was twenty-something years ago, and when I invited you to come to Maui and see us anytime you wanted, I didn't know you were gonna *stay*! But I'm glad you did. It don't matter how old you get—there can never be too many poker pals or too many bad jokes. Which reminds me again . . .

A guy goes to a psychiatrist and says, "Can you help me? My brother thinks he's a chicken."

The shrink says, "Why don't you tell him he's not a chicken?"

And the guy says, "I would, but we need the eggs."

As a good friend, I should probably suggest you quit gambling while you're behind, but please don't. Like the joke says, I can use the eggs. But since I'm running out of ocean-front property for future Woody Harrelson wings, I'll offer you some tips that may help. They're easy to remember:

—Never gamble with a guy named Pops.
—Never eat at a place called Mom's.
—When you're wondering if I'm bluffing, never ever doubt that I can look you in the eye and,

without ever saying a word, convince you to make the wrong call.

How's that for a confidence builder? See ya on Maui. Bring cash.

Willie

P.S. *What did the elephant say to the naked man?*
How do you breathe through that little thing?

MARRIAGE IS A FOUR-LETTER WORD

In an ideal world, a marriage starts with both passion and affection. Lots of marriages survive and can even thrive after one of those is gone. But if you lose 'em both, you may as well turn out the lights, 'cause the party's over.

When I turned fifty, I took stock of my life and thought maybe marriage and me weren't meant to be. I'd been married three times without getting it right. I loved being a dad and being a granddad too. Maybe that was enough—end of story.

But life has a funny way of getting your attention. In January 1986, Waylon, Cash, Kris, and me were shooting a remake of the classic Western movie *Stagecoach*. They all had family members with them, but I was solo and found myself hanging out with the makeup artist, Annie D'Angelo.

Not only was she good-looking and a fair amount of sassy, she was funny too. We hit it off pretty quickly, but it took me some time to convince her I was good marrying material. We did eventually have a nice wedding, but the courtship was long enough that both our young boys were part of the ceremony.

Kris Kristofferson is a great friend of both of us. "We marry what we need," Kris says. "I married a lawyer, and

Willie married a makeup artist!" That's a good line, but in addition to being a great mom, Annie takes on a lot of responsibilities in my world, and there ain't much call for me to wear makeup. I spent years perfecting this face—why cover it up? On the other hand, I do love for her to brush out my long hair.

Either way, thirty-five years after we teamed up, I still look better with Annie at my side. I'm not saying we're perfect; I'm just saying we're close enough.

Despite it taking me a few tries to get the relationship thing right, I'd be the last guy in the world to ask about women. But here are a few things I think work for us.

We share our love for each other and our love for our kids. We share a commitment to peace and to do our part of the work to teach it and to work for it. We share a commitment to the environment of Mother Earth.

You know the old joke:

A married guy's pals ask him if he can play poker all night. "I absolutely can!" the guy says. "But let me ask my wife if I want to."

That joke's probably not a fair comparison, 'cause Annie knows I'm gonna play poker. We see things differently sometimes, but we also listen to one other. We compromise when we need to, but it's more fun when we don't have to. And we've been married so long now that we usually don't have to ask. All it takes is a glance.

We also share a lot of laughs. The past few weeks, we've been taking care of a puppy for Lukas, a really sweet dog that Annie was getting attached to. The night the puppy left with Lukas, Annie seemed sad, so I turned to her at bedtime and said, "If you're missing the puppy around four in the morning, you're welcome to carry me outside to pee."

I like it when she calls me "Babe." And unlike when I was younger, we know how to talk it out when things aren't perfect. One time, we were going back and forth on some problem; I don't even remember what. It was serious, though, 'cause at one point Annie said, "There are worse things than being alone."

My eyes lit up, and I said, "Thank you. I think I'll write that song."

One of the favorite instrumentals I've written is called "Annie." Since it has no lyrics for me to add here, I guess I'll go with the song she inspired. I know she won't take that personally, because there are lots of things worse than being with Annie.

THERE ARE WORSE THINGS THAN BEING ALONE

by Willie Nelson

We finally said all our final goodbyes
And tear after tear fell from everyone's eyes
But just like a funeral where nobody dies
There's worse things than being alone

There are worse things than being alone
Like a full house and nobody home
If the feeling keeps changing then something's gone wrong
And there's worse things than being alone

Well past my halfway in time
But I still have a lot on my mind
And there's one thing for certain beyond right or wrong
There's worse things than being alone

There are worse things than being alone
Like a full house and nobody home
If the feeling keeps changing then something's gone wrong
And there's worse things than being alone

If a feeling keeps changing then something's gone wrong
And there's worse things than being alone

Dear Kids,

When it comes to lucky dads, I hit the jackpot. From my firstborn to my youngest, and to every beautiful one of you in between, my pride for you knows no bounds. I think if someone had asked me when I was younger what kind of family I'd like to have, I might have been smart enough to say a family that is filled with music and a family that lives for love. And here we are.

We're a big clan, the Nelsons—including my bonus daughter Renee, who we lost, but who left us with her beautiful daughter and granddaughter. We also lost our dear Billy, but he is with us still. I've been blessed to live long enough to see you and your kids and their kids turn out so well.

Don't ever forget that we are blessed. Some would say everything is made easy by having a famous father or mother, but we know that a parent's fame can make life harder for kids. I've always believed in my fans and tried to be generous with my time for them. Some of that time was taken from you, but we found our ways to make up for it, and I cherish every moment I've spent with each of you.

You've heard plenty of my advice on life, but maybe this is worth writing down for Nelsons to come, and for anyone else. It all starts with the Golden Rule—with treating others as you'd like to be treated. There's no reason for anyone to go thinking they're special. For every soul on this planet is blessed and deserves love, family, friendship, opportunity, and more, just as we've had.

Sometimes we face hard choices, but remember, the best advice I've ever been given was: "Take my advice and do what you want to."

Doing what we can for others is always a winner. If you see someone who needs help, you help them. Why else are we here? Besides, you can't give it away. Whatever you give away, you get back ten times over.

My mother, Myrle, your grandmother, once wrote a few lines about her beliefs, and I like to think that what mattered for Myrle still matters for all of us. Her creed is filled with optimism, love, and faith in our fellow humans. My favorite part is Myrle writing, "I will eliminate hatred, envy, jealousy, selfishness, and cynicism by developing love for all humanity."

That's a pretty tall order, but we all become better people just by trying to ban negativity from our thoughts and our lives.

In conclusion, please remember that there are three main rules for the Nelson Family: #1. Don't be an asshole. #2. Don't be an asshole. #3. You've got it: Don't be a goddamned asshole.

When in doubt, always choose love, for love is the best way. Love is the only way.

With love,

Willie

P.S. For you and for every kid in the world, it's not too late to save your daddy.

This is one I wrote for my youngest kids, Lukas and Micah.

VALENTINE

by Willie Nelson

Valentine, won't you be my Valentine?
And introduce your heart to mine
And be my Valentine?

Summertime, we could run and play like summertime
With storybooks and nursery rhymes
So be my Valentine

Candy heart
If anyone could, you could have a candy heart
You're the sweetest of all sweethearts
Won't you give your heart to me?
Can't you see?
I love you, valentine
Won't you be my Valentine?
And won't you share your space with mine
And be my Valentine?

Candy heart
If anyone could, you could have a candy heart
You're the sweetest of all sweethearts
Won't you give your heart to me?
Can't you see?
I love you, valentine
Won't you be my Valentine?
And introduce your heart to mine
And be my Valentine?

— ★ ★ ★ —

Dear Santa,

Out of neglect, I may have missed a few years of writing my annual letter to you, but it wasn't because I don't believe in you. You've always been good to me, so I'm not giving up on you—not by a long shot. It's been more than eighty years since I wrote my first letter to you. I said I'd been a good boy, which wasn't entirely true, and I asked for a very special gift, which you, in your wondrous ways, managed to fulfill.

Christmas was always a special time of year for me and for Sister Bobbie. We used to hang stockings on the mantel, and you made sure there was a present in each one on Christmas morning.

Mama used to take Sister and me to Fort Worth at Christmastime, and I'd see you ringing a bell. Our financial status probably could have put us on the receiving end of Santa's donation kettle, but Mama didn't see it that way, and we were always proud to drop in something for those less fortunate than us. Doing that made me happy, and it still does. The first thing you taught me was that the greatest joy is the joy of helping others.

When we were in Fort Worth, I'd see a man who had no legs, who sat on the ground and sang a song as he sold pencils and stationery to Christmas shoppers. I didn't know his name, but I never forgot him. Years later, I wrote a song about him called "Pretty Paper."

After I grew up and had kids, I started playing Santa at

our house. I liked putting on the red suit and the white beard. When my beard started getting white, I only had to put on the suit. Annie's and my son Lukas was born on Christmas Day, and he and his brother Micah gave me more years of filling your big Santa shoes.

All my Santa practice paid off when I got to play a mysterious old gent named Nick in the movie *Angels Sing*. My Nick character—who looked a lot like Saint Nick—had a pretty good take on Christmas traditions when he said that Christmas is what holds families together, across generations and across the distances that separate so many of us these days.

We all know Christmas is the celebration of Christ's birth and is rooted in the messages of love that Christ brought to us. But Christmas and good old Santy Claus have taken on a special meaning of joy, goodness, and giving for people of all faiths, all over the world.

My wish for this Christmas is for everyone to receive some love and to give some love. There's plenty of love to go around. Thanks for helping us share it.

Yours ever so truly,

Nick, I mean Willie

PRETTY PAPER

by Willie Nelson

Pretty paper, pretty ribbons of blue
Wrap your presents to your darling from you
Pretty pencils to write, "I love you"
Pretty paper, pretty ribbons of blue

Crowded street, busy feet hustle by him
Downtown shoppers, Christmas is nigh
There he sits all alone on the sidewalk
Hoping that you won't pass him by

Should you stop? Better not, much too busy
You're in a hurry, my how time does fly
In the distance the ringing of laughter
And in the midst of the laughter he cries

Pretty paper, pretty ribbons of blue
Wrap your presents to your darling from you
Pretty pencils to write, "I love you"
Pretty paper, pretty ribbons of blue

BAND OF BROTHERS

I 'm not sure I ever had good management the first twenty years of my career. Paul could make sure I got paid for my shows, but the record companies would screw you on paper. You could sell a million records and still owe them money after your promotion tour. Waylon said he had a manager who could fix all that, and things got better for a while. But then they got worse.

Lucky for me, there was a smart and dedicated young guy named Mark working for my manager. How dedicated? He took a bum rap and went to jail to protect his boss. That told me he was 100 percent reliable, the opposite of his boss. I heard the warden was a Willie Nelson fan, so I called him up and offered to do a show at the prison. That was a great show for all of us, and while I was there, I mentioned to the warden that Mark was indispensable to my career and tour. Soon after that, they let him go, and Mark Rothbaum became my new manager. We didn't have a contract, and we still don't. Hell, he'd worked for Miles Davis and Waylon Jennings. I figured keeping things moving forward for me would be easy in comparison.

That was over forty years ago, and I can't begin to list all the good things that have happened because of that decision. Sure, sometimes we fight like an old married couple, but it's all good. One time I didn't seem to notice something great

Mark had put together for me. "You could say thank you," he told me.

He had a good point because it can be damn hard to remember to say those magic words. So I said, "Thank you." Then we hugged it out. For good measure, the next morning I called him and thanked him again. Then I called him the next day and the next. After a week of that, Mark said, "I got it. You never have to thank me again."

I never have any doubt about whether he's on my side, so I guess I owe Mark a quick note too.

HEY MARK,

I'm thinking forty years together must be some kind of record. Since we've made it this long, I hope you'll be stuck with me for another forty. Some negative thinkers might assume I won't make it another four decades, but my advice is to not bet against me or Keith Richards. They say every time someone smokes a cigarette, it adds another year to Keith Richards's life. So maybe every time someone fires up a hand-rolled torpedo, it adds another day or week to mine. That means everyone's welcome to burn one for me!

We've come a long ways together. Career-wise, it'd be foolish for any musician to release two hundred albums. You and I both knew that, but I wanted to make as much music as possible, with lots of musicians I love, and you found a way to make it work. Two hundred albums later, we both look pretty smart.

We've had a hell of a run—music, movies, and much more. Thank you for helping make Farm Aid possible. And for making it possible for me to sing to our nation when we were all hurting. Thanks for the world's biggest sixtieth birthday party, then again for my seventieth and my eightieth. It was great to hang out and sing at those shows with Ray Charles, Bob Dylan, Paul Simon, Bonnie Raitt, Leon Russell, Eric Clapton, and lots more talented pals, so I hope you've got something good planned for my ninetieth. And I recommend you start working soon on my hundredth.

Sometimes I think about you, and I just start to laugh.

Remember that time in Baton Rouge when we decided to run to the arena for the show? We ran ten miles in circles till I finally said I was gonna knock on someone's door and ask for help. You said I couldn't knock on a stranger's door. And I said, "I'm no stranger. I'm Willie Nelson."

That homeowner gave us a ride to the gig. That was a great ride, and the truth is, it's all been one hell of a great ride. I'd just like to remind you that the ride ain't over yet.

Back to work!

WE DON'T RUN

by Willie Nelson

We don't run, we don't compromise
We don't quit, we never do
We look for love, we find it in the eyes
The eyes of me and the eyes of you

You are the road, you are the only way
I'll follow you forever more
We'll look for love, we'll find it in the eyes
The eyes that see through all the doors

There is a train that races through the night
On rails of steel that reach the soul
Fueled by fire as soft as candlelight
But it warms the heart of a love grown cold

And we don't run and we don't compromise
We don't quit, we never do
We look for love, we find it in the eyes
The eyes of me and the eyes of you

Words that feel, words that sympathize
Words that heal and understand
Say them now, let them materialize
Say the words throughout the land

We don't run, we don't compromise
We don't quit, we never do
We look for love, find it in the eyes
The eyes of me and the eyes of you

And we don't run and we don't compromise
We don't quit, we never do
We look for love, we find it in the eyes
The eyes of me and the eyes of you

— ✯ ✯ ✯ —

AMERICA THE BEAUTIFUL

I want to take a few moments to highlight some of the things that I love about America. Any list like that would be long indeed, but near the top is the right to speak up and try to make our great democracy even better.

We haven't been perfect, but I do believe we've been the best, and that rather than hiding our flaws, it's best to use our right of free speech and discuss them in the open. When our nation was founded, the great majority of Americans weren't allowed to vote or own property. We had wise founding fathers, but I can't help but think the insights of a few wise founding mothers might have been a good addition.

It took us almost a hundred years to end slavery, and another hundred and fifty years later, we are still struggling with true equality for all. I believe Black Lives Matter. And I believe that Native American Lives Matter. That shouldn't be hard for Americans to understand. Everyone has equal rights. They are inalienable, and no one should be persecuted because of the tone of their skin.

There's a great gospel song with the line "None of us are free if one of us is chained." Every one of us will be stronger when there truly is equal justice and opportunity across our land. That's when every American will know that all lives matter.

I've been asked if I believe people should be allowed to

kneel during the national anthem. Regarding peaceful pro-tests and just about anything else, I believe everyone should do whatever the fuck they want to do. You don't have to watch sports if you don't like the players' personal beliefs. You don't have to attend a gay wedding if you don't want to. You don't have to buy my music, and I ain't gonna change the way I think so you will. We all make our own decisions. I'm trying to make mine with love.

I love this great nation, imperfections and all. I truly hope we can find a way to all come together to talk about our differences and find the right paths to maintain and improve its greatness for generations to come.

DEAR FOUNDING FATHERS,

I hardly know where to begin. You united thirteen colonies, brought us through a trying War of Independence, and shaped our nation through a Constitution that has guided us to this day.

Knowing you couldn't foresee future conditions, the Constitution included a provision that allows it to be amended, but only with great consideration and a nearly unified view of the issue at hand. I've learned over the years from my friends in the White House and the Senate that twenty-six of twenty-seven amendments to the US Constitution have been approved by your lead amendment model, a two-thirds vote by both the House and the Senate, and ratification by three-fourths of the states.

Without our amendments, we wouldn't have the Bill of Rights and would still have slavery. Without our amendments, minorities and women wouldn't be allowed to vote, and neither would eighteen- to twenty-year-olds, young people who were once expected to go to war but denied the right to vote their own conscience.

We've come a long way, but I believe we can do better, especially if we have more women's voices and women in elected office. If there'd been some smart women in the room in 1776, one of them might have pointed out that our nation would never reach its full potential until it considers every person an equal. We're making progress, but we're not there yet.

The Equal Rights Amendment, guaranteeing equal

rights to all regardless of sex, was ratified by two-thirds of the House and Senate, fifty years ago. Thirty-seven states—almost two-thirds—have voted to adopt the ERA. There are arguments on whether all those state votes are still valid, but the way I see it, if you're opposed to women having equal rights, then you're clearly afraid of the competition.

So come on, America! Let's embrace what we know is right—equal rights for all. That includes women. That includes people who fall into many other categories like L, G, B, T, Q, and X. If more letters are needed, they should be included too. Equal rights for all. Full stop. Period. Someday, future Americans will look back at how long this took us and wonder, *What the hell were they thinking?*

And while we're at it, it's time to take a serious look at whether the Electoral College is still serving the greater interests of America. I grew up in Texas believing that our democracy is best represented as one person equals one vote. An amendment to eliminate the Electoral College and elect our president by popular vote would solidify that idea forever.

So, Founding Fathers, you aren't here to help us debate and decide this issue, but you did put these matters in our hands. Let's see if Americans can set politics aside for once and vote for what they know is right.

In the meantime, we are sending love from the twenty-first century. What a long, strange, and fantastic trip it's been.

A proud American,

Willie Nelson

AMERICA THE BEAUTIFUL

by Katharine Lee Bates

Oh, beautiful for spacious skies,
For amber waves of grain,
For purple mountain majesties
Above the fruited plain!
America! America!
God shed his grace on thee,
And crown thy good with brotherhood
From sea to shining sea.

Oh, beautiful for pilgrim feet,
Whose stern, impassioned stress
A thoroughfare for freedom beat
Across the wilderness!
America! America!
God mend thine ev'ry flaw,
Confirm thy soul in self-control,
Thy liberty in law.

Oh, beautiful for heroes proved
In liberating strife,
Who more than self their country loved,
And mercy more than life!
America! America!
May God thy gold refine,

Till all success be nobleness,
And ev'ry gain divine.

Oh, beautiful for patriot dream
That sees beyond the years
Thine alabaster cities gleam,
Undimmed by human tears!
America! America!
God shed his grace on thee,
And crown thy good with brotherhood
From sea to shining sea.

— ★ ★ ★ —

DEAR FOURTH OF JULY,

You and me, we've had some fun together at my little birthday party for America. That term "little" is relative—we had fifty thousand people for the first picnic in 1973, with Waylon, Kris, Leon, John Prine, and Doug Sahm performing in the hot Texas sun. Over the years, we've had a million Americans celebrating your big day.

There are other holidays when the Texas weather is not so hot. Throwing a party for tens of thousands of Texans in some open field can't be found anywhere in a course called Music Business 101. And we rarely make any money. But we all know that our nation's birthday isn't about lining pockets.

Around March, I get cold feet about our hot concert. But when the Fourth rolls around, the buses are lined up backstage as the crowd comes in. It's generally a big bill— sometimes I don't get onstage with the Family Band till early in the morning on July 5.

No matter who the acts are, you're the big draw. The crowd comes for your party, and they often stand in the sun, maybe with a cold beer or mellowed by pot, and soak in the music—a giant melting of American greatness.

Gathering under a sea of red, white, and blue, we remember that we are the same—Americans, not so different from each other or any other people in the world. We laugh, we cry, we like a good joke. We all want freedom, opportunity, and justice for our families, our friends, and our communities.

Those are year-round truths, but once a year we have the opportunity to be reminded of them.

That's the heart of your birthday celebration. Our virtual picnic this year was a great party of its own. I got to do a great set with Lukas and Micah, and we raised funds for some important community work. But I did miss my old friends and their visits on my bus. I missed the crowds, the sunburns, the old folks, the babies, and more.

In 2021, you'll be 245 years old. That's respectable. And I hope we can throw you the party you deserve.

UNCLOUDY DAY

by Willie Nelson

Oh, they tell me of a home far beyond the skies
Oh, they tell me of a home far away
Oh, they tell me of a home where no storm clouds rise
Oh, they tell me of an unclouded day

Oh, the land of cloudless day
Oh, the land of an unclouded sky
Oh, they tell me of a home where no storm clouds rise
Oh, they tell me of an unclouded day

Oh, they tell me of a home where my friends have gone
Oh, they tell me of that land far away
Where the tree of life in eternal bloom
Sheds its fragrance through the unclouded day

Oh, the land of cloudless day
Oh, the land of an unclouded sky
Oh, they tell me of a home where no storm clouds rise
Oh, they tell me of an unclouded day

Oh, they tell me of a King in His beauty there
And they tell me that mine eyes shall behold
Where He sits on the throne that is whiter than snow
In the city that is made of gold

Oh, the land of cloudless day
Oh, the land of an unclouded sky
Oh, they tell me of a home where no storm clouds rise
Oh, they tell me of an unclouded day

Oh, they tell me that He smiles on His children there
And His smile drives their sorrows all away
And they tell me that no tears ever come again
In that lovely land of unclouded day

Oh, the land of cloudless day
Oh, the land of an unclouded sky
Oh, they tell me of a home where no storm clouds rise
Oh, they tell me of an unclouded day

— ★ ★ ★ —

To My Fellow Native Americans,

Dohitsu. That's Cherokee or *Tsalagi* for "How are you?"

To answer my own question, "*Dohi quu.*" I am fine.

My mother, Myrle, gave me my Cherokee blood, and it seems like she and I were both born to wander the hills and plains, as our ancestors had once done. No one taught me those Cherokee words when I was young. I had to look them up. So before my vocabulary runs out, I should explain that, when I was just a crackerjacks kid from small-town Texas, most people wouldn't have pegged me as a future Outstanding Indian of the Year. On the other hand, I did have a good start.

Myrle didn't talk much about her family background when I was little, but even when I was watching my heroes Roy Rogers and Gene Autry at the movies, I had no doubt that the Indians were my heroes too. With few exceptions, those movies didn't do well by America's Indians.

Decades later, we have a better understanding of the injustice done to the indigenous people of our nation, tens of millions of whom once occupied every corner of this great land. In the centuries since the arrival of Christopher Columbus, the lands you lived on, your culture, your language, and your lives were taken in the name of American expansion. You fought heroically, but it's difficult to defeat smallpox and typhus, or overcome modern weaponry and greed.

But here we are, descendants of ancient traditions and adapters of new ones. Together, we are still fighting for justice for every surviving American tribe. I'm just one man, but I've tried to help alleviate some of those injustices. I was deeply touched when, at the 1987 American Indian Exposition in Oklahoma, you named me Outstanding Indian of the Year. I was thrilled when you put that long, feathered headdress on me, and maybe a little less thrilled when you announced that I was going to lead fifteen thousand Native Americans in dance. That is some pressure.

I've been blessed by the opportunity to appear at many other Native American events over the decades, and those experiences have drawn me closer to my Indian heritage. They've helped me understand more about who I am and why I think the way I do.

There's a Navajo proverb that says, "You can't wake a person who is pretending to be asleep." I think we could expand that by saying you also can't wake a person who is pretending to be awake.

For too long, America has pretended not to see a legacy of great injustice. Whether we're aware of our choices or not, we walk through the lives we choose. And the great tragedy of every tribe in America is that the choices were made not by them, but by others who couldn't see the beauty of the people's souls or the debt owed to the caretakers of this land.

Progress for that justice is slow, but I do believe that more and more Americans are waking to past failures. The day is coming when the weight of injustice will be recognized and start to lift, leading us to a time when every Native American can enjoy the fruits of our ancient land and of the full rights and opportunities due to each of us.

There is no word for "goodbye" in Cherokee. Instead, I say, *"Donadagohvi"*—"'Til we meet again."

A HORSE CALLED MUSIC

by Wayne Carson

High on a mountain in western Montana
A silhouette moves 'cross a cinnamon sky
Ridin' along on a horse he called Music
With a song on his lips and a tear in his eye

He dreams of a time and a lady that loved him
And how he would sing her sweet lullaby
But we don't ever ask him, and he never talks about her
I guess it's better to just let it slide

And he sings, "ooh" to the ladies
And ooh he makes 'em sigh
Now he rides away on a horse he called Music
With a pain in his heart and a tear in his eye

Now he rode the Music from Boston to Bozeman
For not too much money, and way too much ride
And those were the days when a horse he called Music
Could jump through the moon and sail across the sky

Now all that's left is an old time-worn cowboy
With nothing more than the sweet by-and-by
Trailin' behind is a horse with no rider
A horse he calls Memories that she used to ride

But he sang, "ooh" to the ladies
And ooh he damn near laid down and died
Now he rides away on a horse he called Music
With a pain in his heart and a tear in his eye

High on a mountain in western Montana
Two crosses cut through a cinnamon sky
Markin' a place where a horse he called Music
Lays with a cowboy in the sweet by-and-by

MAMA, DON'T LET THEM BABIES
GROW UP TO BE PRESIDENTS

I'll admit, it can be fun to look out at my audience and see someone wearing a "Willie for President" T-shirt. Maybe they think I can unite the nation, the way I helped bring the hippies and the rednecks together in the '70s. But there's a huge difference between smoking a joint on the roof of the White House without a care in the world and actually being the occupant of the White House, with the weight of the whole world on your shoulders.

So when someone says, "Willie for President," I generally remind them that my first official act would be to make "bull shit" one word. That usually shuts 'em up.

I've been blessed to meet quite a few presidents, including Jimmy Carter, Ronald Reagan, a couple of guys named George Bush, Bill Clinton, and Barack Obama. In every case, I was impressed by their knowledge and their graciousness and came away with a deeper appreciation of how tough the job must be.

American voters may think that someone being famous means they're smart. When you live in your own reality TV show, for instance, it's easy to think everything will work out. We've seen how good that approach was.

Let's own up to it. The job is hard. The majority of

Americans I talk to already think there's something wrong with the way things are going. There have always been differences, but the differences seem more bitter now. There's a great divide between these thinkers and those thinkers. Everyone thinks they're the ones who are right. But they're not all right, not by a long shot.

"Divide and conquer" has long been a political strategy. If you're the one doing the dividing, you may get to be the conqueror for a while. If you manage to keep dividing, then you're the king. That may feel good, but all would-be kings should remember that this whole glorious American experiment started with us telling a king to fuck off.

There's one thing we can all do, and that's vote. Whether it's in person, absentee, by mail, or online, it needs to be easier to cast a legal ballot. One goal of democracy should be for every legal voter to cast their ballot. Many parents have to work two jobs to make ends meet, so why not make Election Day a national holiday?

The biggest gun we've got is called the ballot box. Vote for the candidates you think will be good for America. And when there are people who've been there too long, or they're doing a terrible job, that's when we have to vote 'em out.

Speaking of which, here's my song on that very subject.

VOTE 'EM OUT

by Willie Nelson and Buddy Cannon

If you don't like who's in there, vote 'em out
That's what Election Day is all about
The biggest gun we've got
Is called "the ballot box"
So if you don't like who's in there, vote 'em out

Vote 'em out (Vote 'em out)
Vote 'em out (Vote 'em out)
And when they're gone we'll sing and dance and shout
Bring some new ones in
And we'll start that show again
And if you don't like who's in there, vote 'em out

If it's a bunch of clowns you voted in
Election Day is comin' 'round again
If you don't like it now
If it's more than you'll allow
If you don't like who's in there, vote 'em out

Vote 'em out (Vote 'em out)
Vote 'em out (Vote 'em out)
And when they're gone we'll sing and dance and shout
Bring some new ones in
And we'll start the show again
And if you don't like who's in there, vote 'em out

DEAR JIMMY CARTER,

I'm writing to say thank you, Mr. President. Thank you for a
lifetime of service to your community, your state, our country, and our world. Thank you for showing us the value of
staying true to who you are. Fifty years of teaching Sunday
school is a great accomplishment on its own. Being governor
of Georgia and president of the United States didn't lessen
that commitment. Neither did your battles with cancer.

I don't think great things happen by accident. Your work
for civil rights in the '60s propelled you to higher office, but
you never forgot what took you there, and your commitment
to helping others never wavered.

Those of us who grew up in small towns in America
know that every person deserves a decent place to live. Your
support of Habitat for Humanity, and your willingness to
show up on a job site with a carpenter's apron and start bang-
ing nails, has inspired millions to join or support that work.
The collective effort from you and all those volunteers has
built thousands of much-needed houses in all fifty states and
all over the world.

It's been an honor to be your friend. It was a thrill to sing
at the White House. Likewise in Stockholm, Sweden, when
you were honored with the Nobel Peace Prize.

I've always loved it when my tour takes me to Georgia,
and I get the opportunity to sing Hoagy Carmichael's beautiful song, "Georgia on My Mind," to the people who love it
most. For five decades, when your schedule allowed during

one of my Georgia concerts, you and Rosalynn have been joining me onstage, and we've been singing "Georgia on My Mind" and "Amazing Grace." For half a century, the crowd has been singing with us, young and old, Republicans and Democrats, brought together by music and the love of a place and faith, and the appreciation of a man who gives his all.

I've always admired a good farmer. I figure that if Jesus' stepfather, Joseph, had been a farmer instead of a carpenter, then Jesus would have been a farmer too. Considering his miracles of the loaves and fishes, think what he could have done with an entire farm!

Sunday school teacher and civil rights activist, husband and father, governor and president, carpenter and farmer—you represent the best that America can be. We could use a lot more like you, but for now I'm just happy we have you.

Give my love to Rosalynn.

Your pal,

GEORGIA ON MY MIND

by Hoagy Carmichael

Georgia, Georgia
The whole day through
Just an old sweet song keeps Georgia on my mind
Georgia
Georgia
A song of you
Comes sweet and clear as moonlight through the pines

Other arms reach out to me
Other eyes smile tenderly
Still, in peaceful dreams I see
The road leads back to you, Georgia
Georgia, no peace I find
Just an old sweet song keeps Georgia on my mind

Georgia, Georgia, no peace, no peace I find
Just an old sweet song keeps Georgia on my mind

Dear Mother Earth,

You've given us all that we need to sustain ourselves. We have what we need to thrive. But somehow, all your bounty is still not enough. There's no part of you that hasn't suffered under our dominion, and the damage we do will affect our children and grandchildren for generations to come.

We could do better. We have science on our side. And our own common sense. But instead, we're distracted by arguments about people over nature, and whether corporations are people.

"Preservation of our environment," said Ronald Reagan in his 1984 State of the Union address, "is not a liberal or conservative challenge; it's common sense."

It's not that complicated. We know people can't thrive unless nature does, but we accept short-term losses for some imagined gains. If we really are stuck with the decision that corporations are people, then it's up to America's and the world's corporate CEOs to start acting like it.

I recently joined with my friends Paul Simon and Edie Brickell (like me, both residents of the Texas Hill Country), to speak out against a natural gas pipeline that was about to be buried beneath the pristine Blanco River. Thousands of voices had been raised, but Paul and I hoped that ours would help persuade the pipeline company to reroute it. With Edie's help, we penned a letter for the pages of the *Houston Chronicle*:

Must we wait until the water is poisoned, the grasslands are gone, the local wildlife extinct and communities ruined before common sense and the love of our land prevails? When will we stop swapping the environment for a profit? To quote a native Hill Country boy, the thirty-sixth president of the United States:

"All my life I have drawn sustenance from the rivers and from the hills of my native state. I want no less for all the children of America what I was privileged to have as a boy," said Lyndon B. Johnson.

It may have been LBJ's words rather than ours that were heard, but the company did respond and shift the path of the pipeline out of the riverbed. There will be more battles to protect our environment, and they will not always be easy. In the words of the late, great John Lewis, that work is "good trouble, necessary trouble."

So, my dear and beautiful Mother Earth, I don't know what to say except that many of us are trying. We know better than to poke our mother in the eye when she's nursing us. We know that it can't be left to others to fight for you. We know a good fight is good for all of us.

We really are trying to get our shit together. And we hope you'll give us enough time.

PO'd in Texas,

Willie Nelson

AMERICAN TUNE

by Paul Simon
(performed by Paul on his album There Goes
Rhymin' Simon, and performed by Willie
on his album Across the Borderline)

Many's the time I've been mistaken
And many times confused
Yes, and I've often felt forsaken
And certainly misused
Oh, but I'm all right, I'm all right
I'm just weary to my bones
Still, you don't expect to be
Bright and bon vivant
So far away from home, so far away from home

I don't know a soul who's not been battered
I don't have a friend who feels at ease
I don't know a dream that's not been shattered
Or driven to its knees
Oh, but it's all right, it's all right
For lived so well so long
Still, when I think of the road
We're traveling on
I wonder what went wrong
I can't help it, I wonder what's gone wrong

And I dreamed I was dying
And I dreamed that my soul rose unexpectedly
And looking back down at me
Smiled reassuringly
And I dreamed I was flying
And high above my eyes could clearly see
The Statue of Liberty
Sailing away to sea
And I dreamed I was flying

Oh, we come on the ship they call the Mayflower
We come on the ship that sailed the moon
We come in the age's most uncertain hour
And sing an American tune
Oh, it's all right, it's all right
It's all right, it's all right
You can't be forever blessed
Still, tomorrow's going to be another working day
And I'm trying to get some rest
That's all I'm trying to get some rest

— ★ ★ ★ —

THE POWER OF POSITIVE
THINKING

That's enough politics. Let's look at something more real. I'm talking about the healing powers of positive thinking, of music, and of time. Look at anything you've ever done, positive or negative, and you'll realize that energy follows thought. Every thought you've ever had is still going around, with some kind of energy behind it. What you say and do in your life are real and have real impacts, both good and bad. So the question is: How do you want to see yourself?

Earlier in the book, I said I'd learned that "a quitter never wins, and a winner never quits." That philosophy was our school motto and was written on the basketball backboard at the Abbott High gym. It may sound corny to you, but to me, it is the ultimate optimism. Early on, it had me thinking, *I can do anything, anywhere.* And all these years later, I feel like I have.

That is visualization and positive thinking. Remember the old song by Johnny Mercer, about accentuating the positive?

My own version of that is "Don't think no negative thoughts." When you put a negative thought into your mind and body, it poisons your system. Worry will make you sick. But I've never seen worrying about something change it.

Instead of always having a worried mind, I decided not to worry.

The alternative to worry is to create a peaceful mind. That peacefulness, combined with visualization, has been key to my life and to my work as a songwriter. If I want to write a great song and find the right way or right person to record it, then also create a way for an audience to hear it, I can't do it through doubt. If I don't eliminate thinking about the difficulty of achieving all that, I may never even start. But if I use my imagination and see myself doing it, that visualization helps make it possible. It helps me transform something I want to do into something that actually happens.

Writing a new song or having some other success can be a great accomplishment, but you have to ask yourself how those stack up against doing good with your life.

Doing good isn't that complicated. Right and wrong are easy choices. We know what to do. And if we think of ourselves as someone who chooses right over wrong, good things will follow.

Goodness and happiness aren't accidental. My friend Bud Shrake was a great pal on and off the golf course. Bud wrote magazine features, wonderful books, and great movies, like our film *Songwriter*. Sometimes when we played golf, Bud would say, "I stayed up late last night writing my Academy Award acceptance speech." He was joking, but it was a joke based in positive thinking. And great things happened his whole life, the last twenty years of which he spent as the beau of Texas governor Ann Richards.

The three of us were friends, and we were united by many things, including our belief in positivity. Ann Richards had little chance of winning a governor's race in Texas, but she ran a positive campaign that cracked open the door, and she kicked it open wide with her great wit.

"Once the shit is out of the bull," she used to say about hot-air politicians, "it's hard to put it back again."

Positive thinking helped Bud and Governor Ann come together at a time in their lives when a lot of people have given up on love. If you believe in the power of positive thinking, then you never have to give up on love.

These aren't hard lessons to learn, but after all these years, I still have to remind myself to envision and create my own happiness. Since no one else can do that for me, I guess I'm writing letters in my own head.

Good morning, Willie. Today is a day for something good.

THE HEALING POWERS OF MUSIC

There truly is a healing power in music. It's a fact. Music is vibrations, and those vibrations reach every part of our being. You may not be able to describe the healing that takes place, but you can feel it because it's real.

Music is our great communicator and our best common denominator. It crosses all boundaries; it brings people together and helps us recognize our common humanity. It doesn't matter if you're a Democrat, Republican, or Independent; what color your skin is; or what language you speak—you probably love music.

Each person listens to the type of music that turns them on, the type of music that makes them feel alive. When we share music we love with others, and they respond to it, we are sharing what we found to be healing.

People travel many miles to hear music they love, to feel the same energy exchange that my band and I feel at every show. When they holler and clap and sing along, it's a great medicine for everyone. The vibrations are all around us, uniting us. That makes music the one thing that can heal us both as individuals and as a people, without any need to become political.

The great power in music can work both ways. And the more people who listen to your music, the more you have to be mindful of that. I loved Leon Russell's music from the first time I heard it, and when he first became well known, I drove to New Mexico for his show.

It was incredible, a big crowd, and Leon had them yelling and screaming. But then he stopped them cold and said, "Listen. Right now, you'd believe anything I said. I won't lead you astray. I'll tell you the truth. But not everyone will do that. You need to be very careful who you let put you in this place. You need to be careful who you give that power to."

From Leon I learned about the responsibilities that come with being a performer with a big following. The two of us were bound by the ideas of why we are here and what we can do with our time on earth.

The tradition of people I loved signing my guitar started when Leon asked me to sign his guitar. He handed me a ball-point pen and said I should scratch the signature into the finish. When I was done, I asked him to sign Trigger the same way. Our mutual respect created an important tradition for me.

Leon and I did hundreds of shows together over the years, but one of the highlights was my seventieth-birthday concert at the Beacon Theater in New York City, where Leon, Ray Charles, and I sang Leon's beautiful "A Song for You." It doesn't get much better than lifting your voices in song with people you love.

Because of music's ability to heal and unite us, my audiences don't hear me talk politics at my shows. We've struck a bargain and have come together to share in the music and the love and the good things that come from it.

That doesn't mean I don't have political views or that I don't express them offstage like any other American is free to do. I believe people are welcome to their opinions, but I also believe in dignity and respect. I believe in people being able to do what they want to do. Not some people—everyone. If people don't like me supporting some political candidate, I don't mind them boycotting my music. That's their call. I might not like their music either.

I find it easy to leave the politics on the bus. I don't want to have anything between me and my audience. When I sing for them, I sing with love, and the people in the audience throw back all that love and energy. It's an ever-expanding circle, and it's been growing since the first time I hit a lick on a guitar onstage as a kid. After all these years, I still don't know of a better medicine.

And that reminds me to say,

"Dear Willie, keep singing."

WHEN WILLIE WENT UP TO HEAVEN

by Willie Nelson and Turk Pipkin

I had a crazy dream the other night
Like when the Devil went down to Georgia
With his fiddle and his pipe.
But this time Willie went up to heaven
And asked Jesus to put things right.
The world is so screwed up, Willie said.
Christ, we need your golden light.
And Jesus said, Hey Willie!
What are you doing here?
You're not due for another twenty years.
Go back home before Saint Peter writes you down
And just keep singing in every city and town.

But we didn't listen, at a very high cost.
We forgot to love our neighbors
And all your labors were lost.
We took the Lord's name in vain.
So I came to fetch you back, Willie cried.
Please save us from the hate we have inside.

Chorus:
What if there's a second coming
But Jesus is afraid to show?
Or what if he does show up
And we're too dumb to know?

Now Jesus's Dad piped up
He puts on quite a show.
And all the angels in heaven listened
As the Lord spoke soft and low.
It's the day the world quit turning.
The day when time stood still
We tried to keep our distance
And we had more than time to kill.
Go back down, my Son, and help them all.
Let Christ be there to catch them when they fall.

But Jesus said, Dad I'm a little scared.
They don't like me down there.
Remember how they settled the score
When I was there before?
I paid the highest cost
And they nailed me to a cross.
Why don't YOU go this time?
And give creation your rhythms and rhymes?
But God said, Son, it's crazy down there
Are you out of your friggin mind?

What if there's a second coming
But Jesus is afraid to show?
Or what if he does show up
And we're too dumb to know?

Go on home, Willie, they both said.
And don't forget the words you can spread
About the Golden Rule, brotherly love
And kindness to strangers.
People whose hearts are right
Are the true world changers.

Thank you, Lord. Thank you, Jesus, Willie said.
Can I ask you one more question?
Are those golden fields of marijuana just ahead?
If they are, I have a suggestion.
Yes, my son, Jesus replied
The pastures of heaven are a heavenly grace.
But if you want a match to smoke it
You'll have to try the other place.
Ha ha ha, Jesus laughed and laughed.
I'm just kidding, he said to Willie
But you should see your face.

LIVE EVERY DAY

On the whole, we're not very good at dealing with death. We don't want to think about it, so for the most part, we don't. Until we have to. Until we lose someone we love. I believe that most people are good people, and it's good people who feel pain the most. In other words, most of us.

Not long ago, a grieving woman told me how hard the loss of her husband had been. "I don't know how to get over it," she said.

Other than with an embrace, I didn't know how to respond. But as we hugged, God gave me an answer. "It's not something you get over," I told her. "It's something you get through."

She considered that, then nodded in agreement, and I think we both felt better. Buddy Cannon later helped me turn that line into a song.

> *Life goes on and on*
> *And when it's gone*
> *It lives in someone new*
> *It's not somethin' you get over*
> *But it's somethin' you get through*

I joke about living another twenty years, but let's face it: we're all gonna die. I may be next, or you may be. Who knows? There's not a lot we can do about it (but if you hear of a long-term cure to death, by all means let me know).

I'm guessing that every one of you has had the same experience I've had, which is to read the morning news and learn that Willie Nelson has died. It seems to be a recurring theme. Quoting Mark Twain, I'd like to say that the reports of my death have been greatly exaggerated.

Those rumors can be scary or hurtful to my family, and that part bothers me. But there is an upside: people have heard so many negative rumors, I figure that when I show up somewhere, everyone will be really glad to see me.

The question is not: Which one of us is going to die tomorrow? The question is: What am I going to do today? Remember my song "Three Days," which helped kicked off this book? There are only three days—yesterday, today, and tomorrow. And there's only one of those we can do anything about. So let's go earn our day. Let's do our best to enjoy life on this side of the dirt.

I don't know what will work for you, but these are things I tell myself: Don't forget to live every day. Remember the Golden Rule, and treat everyone how you want to be treated. Don't forget to breathe deep and get the oxygen flowing to your muscles and your brain. Don't forget to do the things you love. Don't forget to do something for the people you love.

Treat everyone like you want to be treated and
See how that changes your life
Yesterday's dead and tomorrow is blind
And the future is way out of sight
So live every day like it was your last one
And one day you'll be right

Doing my best to live every day helps me to focus on good things to come. There's a huge new audience of young people who've found my music. It makes me feel great to know these old songs are clicking with a whole new crowd. And they know all the words! When I hear a thousand kids singing along to "Bloody Mary Morning," I think, *Y'all weren't even born when that one was written.*

There's a line from a Guy Clark song about having seen the *Mona Lisa*. Like Guy, my life has taken me on some interesting rides. I haven't seen the *Mona Lisa*—guess I was in a hurry when we played Paris—but I've slept in the Lincoln Bedroom, and I've sung in the Rose Garden and at Madison Square Garden. I've sung for saints and sinners in churches and in honky-tonks. I've ridden wild horses and fallen in love with a mule (named Wilhelmina—she was a beauty). I've known the love of wonderful women, and I finally found the one I'd been looking for all along.

I've bet a thousand dollars cash when I didn't have ten. I survived a shoot-out or three and walked away from a plane crash and a bus crash too. Once again, I was lucky, but I also had a good pilot and a great bus driver. I outlasted too many cigarettes and too much whiskey. I wrote a few thousand songs and sang a few thousand more. I've loved my friends, and I've loved all the strangers who became my friends when I played. I've tried to give away some of that love—through hugs, through money, and through the power of my voice, but I learned, as I told my kids, you can't give it away because whatever you put into the world with love comes back a thousand times over.

I did a lot, and I learned a little. And I ain't done yet.

STILL NOT DEAD

by Willie Nelson and Buddy Cannon

I woke up still not dead again today
The internet said I had passed away
But if I die and I wasn't dead to stay
And I woke up still not dead again today

Well, I woke up still not dead again today
The gardener did not find me that way
You can't believe a word that people say
And I woke up still not dead again today

I run up and down the road and makin' music as I go
They say my pace would kill a normal man
But I've never been accused of bein' normal anyway
And I woke up still not dead again today

I woke up still not dead again today
The news said I was gone to my dismay
Don't bury me, I've got a show to play
And I woke up still not dead again today

I run up and down the road and makin' music as I go
They say my pace would kill a normal man
But I've never been accused of bein' normal anyway
And I woke up still not dead again today
Last night I had a dream that I died twice yesterday
And I woke up still not dead again today

Dear Time,

I didn't come here, and I ain't leaving. Besides, you're not so old, and neither am I. Just before this stupid *pandumbic*, I met the great Norman Lear, who is closing in on one hundred and still going strong. We compared notes about our annual birthday counts and both agreed that age is just a number.

As I sing with Toby Keith on my album *First Rose of Spring*, "Ask yourself how old you'd be if you didn't know the day you were born."

My only concern with you, dear Time, is how I want to use you to my advantage. An ideal life is one that's filled with love and laughter.

Speaking of which, did you hear the one about the old man who goes to the pharmacy and asks for some Viagra?

"You're pretty old," the pharmacist says. "How much Viagra do you want?"

The old guy says, "Just enough so I don't roll out of bed."

I have more deep thoughts about the nature of time, rolling around in my brain, but writing them down and sorting them out would diminish the time I have left. So I'm gonna keep it brief and go enjoy some time with Annie instead. With the passing of the years in mind, I've decided to write a little poem just for you, Father Time.

When I was young, I thought I could find perfection
But the older I get, the more I'll settle for an
erection.

Best regards,

Dr. Booger Red

COME ON TIME

by Willie Nelson and Buddy Cannon

Time is my friend, my friend
The more I reject it, the more that it kicks in
Just enough to keep me on my toes
I say, come on time, I've beat you before
Come on time, what have you got for me this time?
I'll take your words of wisdom and I'll try to make 'em rhyme
Hey, it's just me and you again, come on time

Time, you're not fooling me
You're something I can't kill
You're flying like a mighty wind
You're never standing still

Time, as you've passed me by
Why did you leave these lines on my face?
You sure have put me in my place
Come on time, come on time
It looks like you're winning the race

Time, you're not fooling me
You're something I can't kill
You're flying like a mighty wind
You're never standing still

Time, as you've passed me by
Why did you leave these lines on my face?
You sure have put me in my place
Come on time, come on time
It looks like you're winning the race

— ★ ★ ★ —

BRING IT ALL HOME

Okay, friends, we've come a long way from when I was a boy in Abbott. We've shared our time together with a lot of love and a few laughs, and I think I hear my bus warming up down the hill.

When I woke up today, I said to myself, "Good morning, you good-looking devil. You woke up still not dead again today." So that makes it a good morning already. It's not very early, and that's okay. The early bird may get the worm, but the second mouse gets the cheese.

With the day ahead of me, I may go down and check on our pigs. All these years after the Ridgetop farm, I'm a pig farmer once again. This time, Annie and I have partnered with two experts in regenerative farming, Tina and Orion Weldon from TerraPurezza, who are helping us restore soil conditions on the ranch by using pigs, who break up the caliche and rock and fertilize for us. Pigs can make a lot of fertilizer. As my daughter Amy and Arlo Guthrie's daughter Cathy sing in their edgy folk duo, Folk Uke, "Shit makes the flowers grow."

Regenerative farming is a growing movement that can restore depleted farm and ranch lands across America and around the world, and I'm proud to be part of that movement. Also, I've eaten enough bacon and eggs in my time that it's only right that I produce more of my own.

While I'm contemplating breakfast, you may be thinking the drummer's been dragging too long, so what do you say we pick up the tempo just a little, and bring it on home?

My final letters have been on my mind for quite some time. One is to all the songs I love, one is sent on high, one is to my younger self, and at last, there is a letter to the one I love so much and to whom I have always been true.

DEAR WILLIE NELSON'S SONGBOOK,

I first wrote you down and bound you up when I was ten years old. You were a slender thing, but you held all that I'd created, plus the promise of more to come. Over the years and decades, you've grown more portly, and if I assembled you properly, you'd stand ten feet tall! That said, I don't think there's much fat on your bones.

The last few years, I've been lucky to have Buddy Cannon helping me find some of those songs. Sometimes it seems like Buddy and I are sharing one mind—the mind of music. Once I have a starting verse and a melody, I might text it to Buddy, and he adds a bridge and some words of his own. A few texts or emails later, and we have a song.

I don't want you to think that I've finished my work with you here on earth. Buddy and I added nine new songs to you for my *Band of Brothers* album, and the hits just keep coming!

As far as I'm concerned, there's always one more song, and one more idea or story floating above me, waiting to see if I'm paying attention and can match that story with some melody that's rolling through my mind.

I've got one more song to write, and I've got one more bridge to burn. I've got one more endless night. One more lesson to be learned.

See. There's another.

This is the cover and the song list from my first songbook, which I wrote when I was ten years old.

Songbook photographs courtesy of The Wittliff Collections at Texas State University.

Songs / Nelson By
In D E X

ONE MORE SONG TO WRITE

by Buddy Cannon and Willie Nelson

I got one more song to write
And I've got one more bridge to burn
I've got one more endless night
One more lesson to be learned
One more hill to climb
And it's somewhere in my mind
I'll know it when it's right
I've got one more song to write

I got one more horse to ride
And no more secrets left to hide
No more staring at the sun
Just to watch them ponies run
No more bounty to divide
There ain't no secrets left to hide
My life's an open book
Turn the page and have a look

I got one more song to write
I've got one more bridge to burn
I've got one more endless night
One more lesson to be learned
One more hill to climb
And it's somewhere in my mind

But I'll know it when it's right
I've got one more song to write

I got one more song to write
I got one more bridge to burn
I've got one more endless night
One more lesson to be learned
One more hill to climb
And it's somewhere in my mind
I'll know it when it's right
I've got one more song to write

WILLIE NELSON

GOD IS A FOUR-LETTER WORD

No matter your religion, you likely have your own idea of what God is. Some think of God as that Big Guy in the sky who makes all the decisions for us. Some say God is a woman. Some say God is dead. Some say God never was.

My view is simple: I believe that God is love. Period. End of story. For love runs through everyone and everything. Every one of us loves the flowers, and the flowers love the rain. If you love the ocean, you know the ocean lives and loves to caress the shore.

Love is the thing we all have in common. We ache for love. We hope for love. We love and like to be loved. That's God.

*Take these words of wisdom with you
everywhere you go
Tell all the religions in the world
and through them the truth shall flow
But God is love, and love is God
that's all you need to know*

That's a verse from a new song of mine called "God Is Love." When I act with love, I feel that I'm on God's team. What can it hurt to give that a try?

Now, if you're locked onto the idea of the Big Guy in the sky who's listening to our every word, I'd like to be supportive

247

and say I do believe God answers all prayers. But sometimes the answer is no.

Whatever your view of God, here's a note that I hope makes sense to you.

Dear God,

Oh, dear God, I still hope you have a sense of humor. When it's hard to express how bad something is, we tend to say, "Dear God!" But we don't mean it that way. We can't blame you for our failings. None of us are perfect, but we're trying, Lord. Sometimes it may not look that way, but we are trying.

The universe in which we're born is infinitely large, and each of us is so small. We search for meaning when the meaning is all around us, in every moment of our day. We search for you, Lord; we always have. We try to give you a form that we can understand.

You've always been with me, in all your many forms. I started in a Methodist church but found myself at ease with every religion I've tried to understand. I can't tell you now whether I'm a Baptist or a Buddhist. Considering my foot-wear, maybe I'm just a Bootist, a boot-wearing man who believes we were put here for a reason and that by doing our best, we may find the light we seek. If not, our souls are eternal, and perhaps next time around, we'll do better.

You spoke to me in the church. And you spoke to me in the fields and in the open pastures. You spoke to me in the songs of the mockingbirds and blue jays who flew above us. You spoke to me through the rustle of the Texas wind in the trees and through the thunder in the night. And when I pause to listen, you still speak to me.

You spoke to me through the music and the guidance

from Mama Nelson, who told me, "God always prevails because good and goodness can never be defeated."

I wrote a song for you once, called "In God's Eyes," but maybe I wrote all those songs for you. Just as all those songs were gifts from you.

You were with me at the birth of my children, and at the passing of my friends. You are with me when I gaze out on the bluebonnets of Texas. You're with me when the rooster crows at dawn. He doesn't sound sweeter than a mockingbird, but try telling the rooster that.

I feel you when I marvel and wonder at the brilliant rainbows of Maui, when I sing in the little frontier chapel in Luck, and when I stop for reflection on a quiet weekday in the Methodist church where Sister Bobbie and I first lifted our voices to the heavens.

The beauty of this world and the people in it have always been with us. You give us the power to see and smell and touch it. We are born of love, and it is love that carries us through.

Your son of Abbott. Amen!

IN GOD'S EYES

by Willie Nelson

Never think evil thoughts of anyone
It's just as wrong to think as to say
For a thought is but a word that's unspoken
In God's eyes He sees it this way

Lend a hand if you can to a stranger
Never worry if he can't repay
For in time you'll be repaid ten times over
In God's eyes He sees it this way

In God's eyes we're like sheep in a meadow
Now and then a lamb goes astray
But open arms should await its returning
In God's eyes He sees it this way

In God's eyes we're like sheep in a meadow
Now and then a lamb goes astray
But open arms should await its returning
In God's eyes He sees it this way

Hey, folks—here's one that I've been carrying around in my back pocket for a while. It's the letter everyone should write: the letter from you in all your life-found wisdom, written to the younger you, who in my case was more wiseacre than wise.

TO YOUNG BOOGER RED,

Hey, kid, I have a hell of a lot to tell you, but not much time to tell it. I was you once, when I was young and full of piss and vinegar. And now you are me, when I can't piss and still don't like vinegar. And that's okay—after fifty, all men piss in Morse code, anyway.

We created our share of mischief, you and me. Good mischief I like to think. It'd be fun to hook up with some of the old pals and do it all over again. Zeke and Johnny, Waylon and Merle, have all moved on. If missing them would bring them back, I'd miss 'em the whole day long. But missing ain't living, and living works best when you're strong.

I don't want to brag on you, kid, but you turned out okay. I know Mama and Papa and our parents are proud. When you wrote that first song, you saw that other ones might come too. And that's the way I felt when I wrote my latest one. I don't know what the next one will be, but I believe it's gonna be good.

You and me—we had a feeling about reincarnation all along. It just made sense to us. That likely makes both of us a lot older than we know. The older I get, the better I feel about what we've accomplished by believing in the powers of love and music. I don't know if we got it exactly right this time, but we gave it a damn good shot. And we're teed up for another go-round, always striving to get it right.

We still have a lot in common. We both like a good joke, a good game of dominoes, and a good woman too. We didn't know what a saddle felt like till it was strapped on. Or what we looked like till we had our picture took.

You thought you were a fast horse, but a fast horse can't go far. Turns out we are a far horse, after all. Whaddaya say we continue our journey—riding double on a horse called Music as we take in a beautiful Texas sunset?

For now, but not forever, I'm signing off. For this is your old cotton-picking, snuff-dipping, tobacco-chewing, stump-jumping, gravy-sopping, coffeepot-dodging, dumpling-eating, frog-gigging hillbilly from Hill County . . .

Willie Nelson

P.S. Don't forget to type.

GOIN' HOME

by Willie Nelson

The closer I get to my home, Lord
the more I wanna be there
There'll be a gatherin' of loved ones and friends
Lord, you know I wanna be there

There'll be a mixture of teardrops and flowers
crying and talking for hours
'Bout how wild that I was
And if I'd listened to them I wouldn't be there

Well there's old Charlie Toll
they threw away the mold when they made him
And Jimmy McCline it looks like
the wine's finally laid him
And Billie McRae
that I could any day in a card game
And Bessie McNeal
but her tears are real I can see pain

There's a mixture of teardrops and flowers,
crying and talking for hours
'Bout how wild I was, and if I'd listened to them
I wouldn't be there

Lord, thanks for the ride
I got a feeling inside that I know you
And if you see your way
you're welcome to stay
'Cause I'm gonna need you

There's a mixture of teardrops and flowers,
crying and talking for hours
'Bout how wild I was, and if I'd listened to them
I wouldn't be there

Dear Road,

Well here I am, at the end of one road and eager to start down another. They used to say all roads lead to Rome, but they were wrong. All roads lead to another road.

As I finish my letters to America, I'm ready to stand up and get out there with my guitar and my voice and my Family Band and do what I do best. I've said it before, a thousand times, maybe ten thousand, and it always bears repeating.

I still can't wait to get on the road again. 'Cause let's face it, the life I love is making music with my friends, and wherever I go and whatever I do, I just can't wait to be out there with you.

My drivers Tony and Gates have taken me down three million miles of you. They've truly seen it all. Likewise for LG and John, because we travel so far, the drivers have to work in shifts. I don't see everything that passes by, but I feel you stretching out from sea to shining sea beneath our rolling wheels. I smell your fields in bloom and your cities, both shining and sometimes in gloom.

I love you when you take me home, but I love you more when you are stretched out in front of the bus as we make our way to some honky-tonk or concert hall, where people are coming together to hear me play. As I listen to the wheels on the pavement, I can see the faces of my audience, men and women, young and old, white, brown, black, and every shade in between. Americans at their best. Some are coming because they want to feel good and be lifted up, some to forget their troubles or heal their losses. All of them, I hope, are coming to celebrate love and to dance and sing along.

They're waiting for me now. I see them. I hear them. I feel them deep inside. It won't be long now, 'cause I just can't wait to get on the road again.

Everybody sing!

Love,

Willie

ON THE ROAD AGAIN

by Willie Nelson

On the road again
Just can't wait to get on the road again
The life I love is makin' music with my friends
And I can't wait to get on the road again

On the road again
Goin' places that I've never been
Seein' things that I may never see again
And I can't wait to get on the road again

On the road again
Like a band of gypsies
We go down the highway
We're the best of friends
Insisting that the world keep turnin' our way
And our way

Is on the road again
Just can't wait to get on the road again
The life I love is makin' music with my friends
And I can't wait to get on the road again

PERMISSIONS

"America the Beautiful." Lyric by Katherine Lee Bates, 1911 amended version. Public Domain Use.

"American Tune." Words and Music by Paul Simon. Copyright © 1973 (Renewed) Paul Simon (BMI). International Copyright Secured All Rights Reserved. Used by Permission. *Reprinted by Permission of Hal Leonard LLC.*

"Angel Flying Too Close to the Ground." Copyright © 1978 Full Nelson Music. All rights administered by Sony Music Publishing (US) LLC, 424 Church Street, Nashville, Tennessee. Used by permission. All rights reserved.

"Come On Time." Words and Music by Willie Nelson and Buddy Cannon. Copyright © 2019 by Sony Music Publishing LLC and BMG Run Slow Music. All Rights on behalf of Sony Music Publishing LLC Administered by Sony Music Publishing LLC, 424 Church Street, Suite 1200, Nashville, TN 37219. All Rights on behalf of BMG Run Slow Music Administered by BMG Rights Management (US) LLC. International Copyright Secured All Rights Reserved. *Reprinted by Permission of Sony Music Publishing, LLC and Hal Leonard LLC.*

"December Day." Copyright © 1968 Sony Music Publishing (US) LLC. All rights administered by Sony Music Publishing (US) LLC, 424 Church Street, Nashville, Tennessee. Used by permission. All rights reserved.

"Family Bible." Copyright © 1980 Full Nelson Music. All rights administered by Sony Music Publishing (US) LLC, 424 Church Street, Nashville, Tennessee. Used by permission. All rights reserved.

"Funny How Time Slips Away." Copyright © 1961 Sony Music Publishing (US) LLC. All rights administered by Sony Music Publishing (US) LLC, 424 Church Street, Nashville, Tennessee. Used by permission. All rights reserved.

"Georgia On My Mind." Words and Music by Hoagy Carmichael and Stuart Gorrell. Copyright © 1930 by Peermusic III, Ltd. Copyright Renewed. All Rights Reserved. *Used by Permission.*

"Goin' Home." Copyright © 1971 Full Nelson Music. All rights administered by Sony Music Publishing (US) LLC, 424 Church Street, Nashville, Tennessee. Used by permission. All rights reserved.

"Healing Hands of Time." Copyright © 1964 Sony Music Publishing

ABOUT THE AUTHORS

From a small town in Texas to international acclaim as a singer, songwriter, actor and activist, gambler and joker, Willie Nelson's career has topped the worlds of country and popular music with frequent forays in film, television, and literature. He has been honored with thirteen Grammy Awards, The Library of Congress Gershwin Prize, and the Kennedy Center Honors. His populist activism has supported environmental and Native American causes, legalization of cannabis, and America's Family Farmers.

Turk Pipkin has published a dozen books, including *The Tao of Willie*, also coauthored with his friend Willie Nelson. He is also known for his roles in two HBO series, *The Sopranos* and *The Leftovers*, and is the cofounder of the global education nonprofit, The Nobelity Project. In forty years, he has never beat Willie in dominoes.